FBC
3 –
6/22

Interpreting the Aging Self

Harry J. Berman, Ph.D. is professor of Child, Family, and Community Services at Sangamon State University in Springfield, Illinois, where he teaches courses on life span development and aging. He received a doctorate in psychology from Washington University, St. Louis, and has also been on the faculty of The Pennsylvania State University. He has published research on retirement decisions, relations between adult children and aging parents, the turnover of nurse aides in nursing homes, and personal journals of later life.

Interpreting
THE
Aging Self

Personal Journals of Later Life

Harry J. Berman, PHD

Springer Publishing Company

Springer Publishing Company, Inc.
536 Broadway
New York, NY 10012-3955

Cover design by Tom Yabut

94 95 96 97 98 / 5 4 3 2 1

Library of Congress Cataloging-in-Publication Data

Berman, Harry J.
    Interpreting the aging self : journals of later life / Harry J. Berman.
        p. cm.
    Includes bibliographical references and index.
    ISBN 0-8261-8060-4
    1. Old age—United States—Case studies. 2. Authors, American—20th century—Diaries. 3. Aged—United States. I. Title.
HQ1064.U5B3745   1994
305.26'0973—dc20   94-23168
                                                              CIP

Printed in the United States of America

For Nanny

May her memory be for a blessing

Permissions

Contents

Acknowledgments

I wish to acknowledge the support of Sangamon State University in the preparation of this book. I received a sabbatical during the 1991–1992 academic year and, through Sangamon State's Institute for Public Affairs, received additional released time to aid me in completing this work. My colleagues in the Child, Family and Community Services Program and the Central Illinois Philosophers Group have provided much appreciated encouragement. I especially want to thank Professor Sheldon Tobin, who provided a valuable critique of the manuscript and strongly encouraged the incorporation of humanities perspectives in gerontology during his tenure as editor of *The Gerontologist*. I also want to thank individuals who have read portions of the manuscript, provided helpful suggestions, or offered strong encouragement to carry out this project: David Gutmann, Bertram Cohler, Larry Shiner, and Sylvia Sieferman. Elisabeth McPherson read the entire manuscript and provided excellent and very constructive suggestions. I am especially indebted to my wife, Deborah McPherson Berman, who edited the entire manuscript. Her love and moral support have sustained me throughout this project, and her editorial skills have considerably enhanced this work.

Foreword

Writing a foreword to this masterful book after its reading is like savoring dessert and a fine brandy following a gourmet dinner. It is indeed a book of rare delicacy that offers much food for thought. The author, Harry J. Berman, relates introspective personal narratives of five well-known writers to various theories of human development. This allows readers of this book to feast on the words of articulate writers, while contemplating how interpretations of their personal writings are congruent with theoretical formulations of the self.

The five writers discussed provide sensitive, and often brilliant, portrayals of their lives and experiences as they are confronted by vicissitudes and adversities in the latter half of life. Dr. Berman intersperses passages from their journals and diaries with his own insights and interpretations of possible meanings, allowing the reader to achieve an empathic resonance with each diarist. Too often, as scientists who seek to develop theories with common denominators in human behavior, we do not capture a true sense of the human experience. This is not so here. Dr. Berman highlights the essence of experienced lives. That is what makes this book so special.

Berman does not choose to draw on all available theories but rather selects from among those of a psychodynamic nature. He uses theories of personality to make sense of internal dialogues and their meanings. Among others, he discusses Daniel Levinson's conception of adult development, attachment theory, Erik Erikson's last crisis of ego integrity versus despair, developmental constructivism that posits meaning-making as the central activity of human beings, and the struggle toward individuation of Carl Jung. His discussions of how selected theories apply to the diarists' writings of their personal experiences and their selves are surely insightful, but not to be minimized is how these didactic excursions offer the opportunity to use real lives to explicate theory. A bonus for me was the ruminative pleasure I experienced when thinking of additional theories of development. I felt a tacit encouragement to play with ideas regarding the contents of personal narratives, their interpretations and relevant theories. Scholars from the humanities, I am sure, would also appreciate and enjoy this cognitive process that emanates from the richness of studying the personal writings of articulate, introspective authors. It is truly an interdisciplinary treatise.

Rare indeed is the author who is able to synthesize and analyze material from more than one discipline. More common is multidisciplinary collaboration [i.e., when experts from two or more disciplines approach or investigate a shared phenomenon from their separate perspectives]. The true interdisciplinarian aspires to bridge multiple disciplines. These interdisciplinary scholars risk criticism from others who are threatened by the encroachment of someone from another discipline on their territory. We professors, especially those with gerontological interests, know only too well how disciplinary terrains are carefully guarded. I experienced this treatment firsthand when an anthropology student who sought my counsel to develop her doctoral dissertation could not have me on her committee because the chair of her department said that I was not an anthropologist. Subsequently, I had to write innumerable letters, as Editor-in-Chief of *The Gerontologist*, explaining to tenure committees that candidates who publish in multidisciplinary peer-review journals are not abandoning their disciplines. One candidate, a splendid junior investigator, requested that in my letter I use the word psychologist "at least sixteen times and avoid gerontologist." In turn, had a junior colleague written Harry Berman's book, some senior colleagues in the department would fault his or her straying from the straight and narrow. With disbelief, because I come from a tradition of crossing disciplines, I have watched articles published in disciplinary journals weighed several tons heavier than articles in multidisciplinary journals, and even weightier than books. It is common for senior faculty members to advise junior colleagues, "Get your articles into *our* journals and later you can do those other things." A student once responded to this advice by saying that he did not want to be a technician first and thinker later. This book is written by an interdisciplinary thinker, one who has put ingredients from diverse disciplines into his mixing bowl and has concocted a mouth-watering recipe for all of us.

Surrounding the five chapters that focus on the diarists' narratives are splendid introductory and final chapters containing clarifications of words, phrases, and constructs in the broad gerontological lexicon including the distinction between emic (in the words of the sayer) and etic (the interpretation of the words); the meanings of the terms diary, journal, and personal journal; the self-as-knower (or self-as-subject) and the self-as-known (or self-as-object); hermeneutics and human science. But there is much more in this scholarly offering. A precision shines through that is greatly appreciated by me, a busy social scientist who has too much on his plate to sufficiently reflect on the connotations of constructs I use and are used by others, constructs such as "interpretation of meanings" and "the self."

Still, it is my belief that Berman's important contribution

resides in how personal narratives challenge us to use, to assess, and to develop theories of human development salient to the lives of people as they are lived and experienced in the latter half of life. This challenge should not be taken lightly. It should also be taken with a thirst for understanding the human condition and with an appetite for interdisciplinary connectedness.

SHELDON S. TOBIN, PhD

Preface

I am a psychologist by training and teach courses on lifespan development and the psychology of aging. When I first started teaching 20 years ago, I was distressed by what I felt was the absence of older people themselves from research on the psychology of aging. The psychology of aging of that era consisted mostly of studies on the classic topics of psychology, such as intelligence, learning, memory, and reaction time, with an "aging variable" thrown in. I understand now that such studies were needed to establish basic information about the processes of aging and to create credibility with biologists and other psychologists for the nascent field of geropsychology. But at the time, I resented the way that geropsychology, the branch of learning that should be most concerned with the sense that people make out of their own aging, seemed to treat the subjects of research purely as objects, rather than as experiencing beings who might themselves have something useful to say about what was happening to them. I became committed to the idea of somehow bringing the experience of aging into the teaching of the psychology of aging and, of equal importance, into the field of gerontology.

Of course, the intellectual ground for such thinking was

also part of the *Zeitgeist* of that era. Like many graduate students of the early 1970s, I was caught up in the emerging critique of positivism and the increasing prominence of the idea that what we can claim to know is not exhausted by what is traditionally understood to be the method of science. My exposure to the critique of positivism was through my association with Richard de Charms, who taught me about the philosophical foundations of psychology and who introduced me to the work of Michael Polanyi.

In response to my misgivings about the seeming absence of older people from the psychology of aging, I turned to literature as a source of "data" about the experience of aging and, particularly, to published diaries written by older people. Over the years I have presented separate papers on several such diaries. In this book, I have revised and expanded these papers, added new material, and attempted to present the diaries not so much within a framework but, rather, within a set of contexts: the philosophical tradition of hermeneutics, ideas from literary criticism, and the history of the use of personal documents in psychology.

Much has happened in geropsychology and in intellectual life over the past 20 years. In this postmodern, paradigm-switching era, unreconstructed positivists are hard to find. Gerontologists have moved from being preoccupied with studies of basic psychological processes to attempting to grapple with broader questions, such as the stresses of caring for aging parents and of being cared for by one's children, the nature of wisdom, and how older people sustain a sense of life's meaningfulness. Nonetheless, the integration of what Sartre called the *universal singular* as realized in literature into the discipline of gerontology is in its early stages. This book is intended as a contribution to that end.

HARRY J. BERMAN

Introduction

When a question arises, it breaks open the
being of the object.
(Gadamer, 1960/1992, p. 363)

The work described in this book originates in this question: What is it like to be an older person? The question seems simple. Each of the words is readily understandable and its grammatical form is straightforward. Yet the mere asking of this question raises issues that go to the heart of our lives as gerontological researchers.

The words "to be" in the question "What is it like to be old?" imply that the answer must be given in terms of descriptions of experience (being), rather than in terms of explanations of causes. The word "like" implies a process of interpretation, a series of linguistic approximations and metaphors, rather than objective measures.

Perhaps for these reasons—that the question calls for description rather than explanation; words and metaphor, rather than measurement—the question "What is it like to be old?" should be declared off limits, beyond the pale, *verboten*, as far as the serious, scientific work of gerontologists is concerned.

But what a loss that would be. Surely, among the many important things that gerontologists should be able to convey to our audiences of students, policymakers, and the general public is the sense of what it is like—what it means—to be old in this day and age.

Rather than abandon the question, I have grounded it in a line of thinking that centers on the investigation of lived experience and holds as its central assumption that the essence of human being is making meaning. To provide answers to the question, I have used published personal journals (diaries) written in later life. Personal journals are particularly suitable sources of information about what it is like to be an older person, because in them authors attempt to fixate the meaning of the day-to-day flow of experience. These diaries are effective at capturing the mood of the moment, but they also go beyond the moment and embed the flux of experience in larger contexts of meaning.

Reading personal journals of later life has the character not of simply assimilating what is in them, as might be the case with reading a newspaper, but rather the character of an experience or a significant encounter. The encounter with these texts leads to a form of self-disclosure in the sense that they reveal to the reader aspects of his or her own way of being that may have gone unobserved. May Sarton has written humorously about the effects her journals have had on their readers. Throughout the later journals, there are references to letters she receives from readers who have been moved by these works. In *Encore* she reflects on the kind of influence she has had. She distinguishes between her journals and the plethora of how-to books that are on the market. As we might expect from such a fiercely independent person, she is highly scornful of self-help books and thinks people who read them are crazy. "I cannot imagine making a step-by-step analysis of how to live in solitude" (p. 214). Nonetheless, she recognizes that her books have changed people's lives. The influence seems to arise through the mere description of her way of life.

> The other day I got a charming letter, one that feeds me as much as any I have ever had because it is such a simple kind of in-

fluence that I am told I wielded in this case. It is from a woman who decided after reading *The House by the Sea* that she would go and buy a bird feeder and set it up, perfectly confident that birds would come. Of course they might not have, but lo and behold, the next day there were every sort of bird you can imagine, birds I had described—chickadees, bluejays, nuthatches, and God knows what. And isn't it delightful that if I am asked, "Do you influence people?" I can answer, "I influenced someone to buy a bird feeder." (p. 214)

In my own case, Sarton's passion for having flowers in her house as often as possible has awakened a similar desire in me. Prior to reading Sarton, I didn't know what I was missing.

More encompassing, however, than augmenting one's life with birds and flowers is the opportunity afforded by these texts to observe how people have met the challenges of later life and how they have responded to suffering. As Frankl (1959) has observed, the attitude we take toward unavoidable suffering is one of the linchpins of maintaining a sense of the meaningfulness of life. In this sense, personal journals are potentially emancipatory. By entering into internal dialogue with these texts, readers can be freed from simplistic, habitual ways of thinking about later life and even be aided to find meaning in suffering.

We can think about the potential impact of reading published personal journals on gerontology students, on service providers, on nonprofessional adult readers, and on older people themselves. For students who may have little experience with the aged, diaries offer an opportunity to be exposed to the lived worlds of older people as they are recounted over an extended period of time. As Van Manen (1990) has noted, one outcome of hermeneutic phenomenological research in general is the expansion of thoughtfulness and the ability to act toward others with tact. This would certainly hold true in regard to the impact on gerontology students of studying journals of later life. Particularly relevant in this regard are the descriptions of the rise and fall of hope as Sarton struggled with her multiple illnesses in *Endgame* and *Encore* or the recovery from despair over the course of a year documented in Grumbach's *Coming into the End Zone*.

For current service providers, the journals offer an opportunity to have a sustained encounter with a thoughtful older person, an encounter that is not shaped by what could be termed technical considerations, such as filling out a form to determine the need for services, leading an activity, or taking blood pressure. For the service provider, the diarist is neither a case to be managed nor a client to be served but simply an older person to be encountered. Interestingly, the journals give occasional glimpses to service providers of what it is like to be served and of how easy it is for service providers to adopt unintentionally a patronizing attitude toward their clients. This comes through especially strongly in a description Grumbach offers of her encounter with a young nurse in a doctor's office.

For nonprofessional adult readers, the journals can serve as a means of anticipatory socialization. For the most part, later life is *terra incognita* for young and middle-aged adults. The journals open up a range of possible future selves. They can suggest activities that should be undertaken in early and middle adulthood to enrich the later years.

Finally, for older people themselves, the published journals can serve as windows and mirrors. They can open up new views of the possibilities of later life. They can offer new interpretations of the situations older people find themselves in, even if those situations are fraught with difficulty. As Storr (1988) has put it, the human mind is so constituted that a new balance or restoration within the subjective imaginative world is felt as if it were a change for the better in the external world. Reading a journal will not change an older person's circumstances, but it may change the way an older person feels about those circumstances. Journals can also provide articulations for older people of feelings they have had but may not have been able to express. Such articulations of their own experience can be powerfully affirming and lead to the sense that their feelings are true or valid and perfectly normal.

In addition to their value for students, service providers, and general readers in middle and later adulthood, published personal journals are a form of autobiographical writing that ought to have a place in the scientific study of human development. One of the aims of this book is to consider the sense in which personal journals can be construed as admissible evidence into scientific discourse about developmental processes.

There has been increasing interest among developmentalists in the use of autobiographical materials, particularly in the collection and analysis of life histories. Works by Kotre (1984), Kaufman (1986), McAdams (1993), and Gubrium (1992) typify the surge of interest in getting people's stories in their own words. Within psychology, this interest constitutes a harking back to the personological tradition of Henry Murray; within sociology, it amounts to a revival of the tradition of the Chicago School of the 1920s and 1930s.

Along with increasing interest in autobiographical accounts, in this era of the "reconfiguration of social thought" there has been a continuing call for the incorporation of the materials and perspectives of the humanities into the field of gerontology. A landmark in the history of the effort to establish the relevance of the humanities to the study of aging was the recent publication of the *Handbook of Aging and the Humanities* (Cole, Van Tassel, & Kastenbaum, 1992), published by Springer Publishing Company.

What is common both to the renewed interest in autobiographical materials and to the call for incorporation of the humanities into gerontology is an inevitable grappling with the matter of meaning. Research on personal meaning will be discussed in Chapter 6, but at this point it is worth noting that the kind of meaning at stake in both the study of autobiographical materials and the humanities is existential meaning, the answers that people provide to questions about life's meaning and what makes life meaningful. In telling their life stories, people are drawn into consideration of the meaning of their lives. Existential meaning is also a central concern of the humanities.

The present work, focusing as it does on published diaries, is related both to the body of research on autobiographical materials and to the attempt to build bridges between the humanities and the social sciences. And, as with other studies of autobiographical materials and works of the humanities, we will be drawn repeatedly into a consideration of existential meaning. All of the diarists considered are struggling in their own ways to articulate the meaning of their lives.

The first chapter of this book considers three topics that form the conceptual background to this work—the emerging approach to psychological inquiry known as human science, the long tradition of studying personal documents in psychology, and the recent attempts to constitute a hermeneutic gerontology.

The second chapter addresses considerations related to the diary as a literary form, including the relation between diaries and the Western tradition of individualism and the recent surge of interest in diaries among literary critics.

Following these introductory chapters are five chapters on particular personal journals of later life, those of Elizabeth Vining, May Sarton, Doris Grumbach, Alan Olmstead, and Florida Scott-Maxwell. Each of these chapters is organized into the same three sections. The chapters begin with biographical profiles of the journal authors. Next, the principal themes in the journals are presented. Finally, interpretations of those themes are offered. This organizational structure is intended to reflect an approach to these texts in the spirit of hermeneutic dialogue. To the extent possible, the text is initially grasped in its own terms. Then the emergent understanding of the text is applied to the reader's concerns.

Following the five chapters on the works of individual diarists, Chapter 8 considers the concept of self and how it relates to the personal journal. This chapter also includes a further discussion of the seven journals of May Sarton, which constitute a uniquely valuable body of material because of the length of later life that they span and the compelling accounts of ordinary struggles they contain.

The book concludes with a chapter discussing the implications of the study of personal journals for our ideas about what constitutes knowledge of aging.

Of the five authors whose journals are considered in this book, four are women and one is a man. Whether this gender distribution accurately reflects the proportion of journals of later life published by women and by men—or the proportion of journals of later life written by women and by men, but unpublished—is not known with any degree of certainty. However, it does seem that the preponderance of journals of later life are those of women. There are a variety of reasons why this may be so. One is the fact that there are more women than men in later life; another may be merely the vagaries of the publishing industry. Nonetheless, it is interesting to speculate about other factors that may be at play in creating a gender disparity. As one feminist literary critic has argued (Benstock, 1988), there seems to be an inherent congruity between the journal form, with its discontinuity and disavowal of a strict coherence in the presentation of the self, and women's experiences of marginalization and multiple role demands. Exploration of this idea awaits further study.

In interpreting the texts my intention was to examine their themes in light of concepts and theories from gerontology and developmental psychology. I see this process as a kind of dialogue in which the texts put questions to the theories and the theories put questions to the texts. Because the most telling material in the journals deals with issues of meaning, the

relevant concepts and theories from gerontology and developmental psychology are also those that deal most directly
with meaning. Consequently, there is considerable emphasis on interpreting the texts using ideas put forward by psy-
choanalytically oriented thinkers: Freud, Jung, Rank, Erikson, Levinson, and Gutmann. As Judith Viorst has put it,
"[W]ith all of its imperfections, the psychoanalytic perspective offers the most profound insights into what we are and
why we do what we do" (1986, p. 1).

As will be elaborated in Chapter 2, the texts selected for
inclusion in this book are all *personal* journals, that is, the
life of the author is the prime subject. This is in contrast to
journals whose principal focus is on topics such as travel or
gardening. In addition, the journals considered in this book
were all written by older authors, ranging in age from 59 to
85. Thus, they are *personal journals of later life*. The works
included here are not the only published personal journals
of later life, although they are particularly good examples of
the genre. Published diaries written by Malcolm Cowley, Joyce
Horner, Alice James, and Anne Truitt are among those that
should be considered in future research in this area. In addition, I hope that the acknowledgment of the importance of
these texts will spur the publication of other diaries of later
life. From my conversations with people about this book, it is
clear to me that there are many valuable diaries written by
older people sitting unread in desk drawers. Gathering, editing, and publishing these works would be a valuable activity
in its own right, on a par with recent efforts to obtain, archive,
and disseminate oral histories.

We turn our attention now to the conceptual underpinnings
of research on personal journals of later life, the traditions
out of which this book emerges. As we take up the issues to
be considered in Chapter 1—the idea of human science, the
history of the use of personal documents by psychologists,
and attempts to establish a hermeneutic gerontology—in the
background will be concerns about whether and in what way

this enterprise can be viewed as research, in what sense the analysis of personal journals is scientific, and, most important of all, what kind of knowledge of aging is provided by the study of personal journals of later life. This key question is the one to which we will return at the end of the book after having considered each of the journals.

Human Science and the Use of Personal Documents

1

Despite the enormous growth of research on the psychology of aging, what we understand about day-to-day experience in later life is still very limited. In many respects, the inner lives of older people continue to constitute a kind of *terra incognita*. Our limited knowledge of the inner lives of older people is largely due to the dominance of early twentieth century positivism over late twentieth century behavioral and social science. Under the axioms of the positivistic philosophy of science as adopted by psychology and sociology, acceptable data, scientific evidence, and, in the extreme, knowledge itself are confined to that which has been generated from potentially replicable public operations using measurable concepts (Bridgman, 1927). Consequently, a topic such as the "experience of aging" would be viewed as impossible to approach scientifically and, therefore, unworthy of consideration.

However, critical examinations of the assumptions of logical positivism have resulted in what Geertz (1980) has termed a "refiguration of the social sciences" and a reconsideration of previously excluded areas of research. One line of criticism arises from the philosophical tradition known as hermeneutic phenomenology, or, more simply, human science, and originates in the writings of the philosophers Husserl, Heidegger, Gadamer, and Ricoeur. Among those who have worked to develop the human science position in psychology are Giorgi (1970), Pocklinghorne (1983), Messer, Sass, and Woolfolk (1988), and Packer and Addison (1989).

The central tenet of the human science perspective is that humans are self-interpreting animals. Human science asserts that the customs, the institutions and, most significantly, the language of a given culture channel and constitute human experience. Even what we usually refer to as the self is largely determined by the possibilities laid open to us by language and culture (Shotter & Gergen, 1989). Moreover, such culturally constrained experience is not transparent to itself. It is a kind of text analog, an intrinsically obscure object that is constantly interpreted to bring to light its meaning (Sass, 1988). The subject matter of human science is, therefore, lived experience, understood as individuals' experiences cast into language (i.e., interpreted) by means of culturally available meanings.

To establish the ground for the approach adopted in this book, this chapter begins with a discussion of the origins and implications of the term human science and considers what it means to do human science research.

The idea that lived experience is an acceptable subject matter for research has led to interest in personal documents in which people create texts that capture their own lived experience. Examples of personal documents are collections of letters, memoirs, autobiographies, and diaries. However, psychological research using personal documents did not begin with the current critique of positivism. Rather, personal documents figured prominently in the work of psychologists of an earlier era. This chapter will also provide a historical perspective on the use of personal documents in psychology.

The field of geropsychology came of age under the guiding light of positivistic science. The idea was to build a science of aging under the narrowest of definitions of science. Over the years, however, certain gerontologists have railed against the absence in gerontology of the study of the personal meaning of aging and have engaged in research that values the investigation of lived experience. This chapter will also briefly identify those gerontologists and will highlight recent contributions to the nascent human science perspective in gerontology.

HUMAN SCIENCE RESEARCH

Human science research involves the interpretation of texts and text analogs. The preferred methods of natural science involve detached observation, controlled experiment and quantitative measurement. In contrast, the preferred methods of human science involve description of texts, interpretation, and self-reflective or critical analysis. Natural science taxonomizes and explains; human science explicates meaning. Human science research methods involve particular researchers' encounters with texts and text analogs with the aim of producing historically and culturally rooted reflections on lived experiences.

The world of lived experience is both the source and object of human science research (Van Manen, 1990). There are various approaches to gathering or collecting lived-experience material. Although the concept of data has quantitative overtones deriving from positivistic science, originally the term *datum* meant something given or granted. In natural science, data are drawn out of the objects of research. In contrast, human science uses data in the original sense of the term, that which has been given by subjects (i.e., self-interpreting beings).

Just as in natural science, human science involves a process of reasoning about data. In the natural sciences reasoning involves the processes of induction and deduction so familiar to us from standard research methods courses. In the human sciences, reasoning involves a process of articulating meaning by focusing on the dialectical relationship between parts and wholes (Burke, 1992; Gadamer, 1960/1992, p. 223). To assert that meaning inevitably involves reasoning about parts and wholes is to assert that meaning is contextual. Interpretation occurs within a circle in which parts are always interpreted within some understanding of the whole, which is in turn understood by coming to understand its constituent parts (Woolfolk, Sass, & Messer, 1988). A fact does not stand on its own independent of the context or interpreter but rather is partially constituted by them. The dialectical relationship between parts and wholes, which encompasses the relationship between knower and known, is referred to as the hermeneutic circle. What we understand is based on what we already know and what we already know comes from being able to understand.

Part-whole reasoning is central to the work of literary and art critics, historians and cultural anthropologists. Critics attempt to interpret works of art or literature by analyzing them into their parts and showing how they relate to the whole. But the parts themselves arise out of the whole of the work. Historians attempt to find significant coherences in traces from the past. The coherences emerge from and then give order to the separate traces. Cultural anthropologists attempt to describe cultures by moving back and forth between specific artifacts and practices and larger structures of meaning. As Geertz (1973), an anthropologist working in the human science tradition, has put it, the process of doing interpretive research involves "a continuous dialectical tacking between the most local of local detail and the most global of global structures in such a way as to bring both into view simultaneously" (p. 239).

Recently published volumes of human science research (Packer & Addison, 1989; Thomas, 1989) exhibit the range of methods of gathering data that can be used to yield understanding of lived experience. Thomas's collection includes analysis of written texts, participant observation, intensive case studies, and in-depth interviews. Packer and Addison's volume (1989) includes participant observation, case studies, audio and video recordings, and interviews. To these sources of data, Van Manen (1990) adds lived-experience descriptions, the tracing of etymological sources and idiomatic phrases, experiential descriptions in literature and biography, and experiential descriptions in diaries or journals. It is the latter as a source of data about the experience of aging that is the subject of this book.

The approach to the study of personal journals of later life in this book consists of close reading, the isolation and description of themes, and the interpretation of those themes in light of psychological concepts and developmental theories.

Reading Journals

Human science posits that all knowing is related knowing, that is, knowledge arises out of a relationship between the text and the reader. Accordingly, it is helpful to try to characterize the reader's (i.e., researcher's) experience in doing the kind of reading required for human science research.

Wertz's (1984) description of the phenomenological method can be helpful to characterize the approach to be taken in analyzing personal journals. The reading begins with a bracketing or suspension of preconceptions and an immersion in the lived reality or world that the text makes visible. In describing the change that aging has brought about in her reading habits, Grumbach (1991) unwittingly provides an excellent characterization of this method of reading:

> It is hard work to read more slowly . . . [W]hen I slow down, I interlard the writers' words with my own. I think about what they are saying, I consider their methods, I hesitate before their choices, I dilly-dally in their views instead of racing through their styles and subject matter. (p. 15)

Allport (1942) has also provided a description of this initial phase of the encounter with a personal document: "The only reasonable thing to do if one wishes to study a phenomenon is to put a specimen before one's eyes and look at it repeatedly until its essential features sink indelibly into one's mind" (p. 143).

The process of reading personal journals can be understood by analogy with the encounter between clients and therapists. The journals are a continuing report of life in the present, regardless of when that present was. The reader sees the days unfold much as a therapist would during a year of therapy. The analysis of the journals depends on being open to the feelings aroused by these texts as a basis for grasping the world of the other, much as therapists use the feelings generated by clients in them (i.e., counter transference) as therapeutic tools.

Isolating and Describing Themes

The purpose of hermeneutic phenomenological reflection is to try to grasp the essential meaning of something (Van Manen, 1990, p. 77). As Van Manen (1990) has noted, to grasp meaning is both easy and difficult. People are always relating to the world in terms of the meanings they impart to events, but the explication of meaning is not straightforward.

To grasp its meaning, it is helpful to think of approaching a text in terms of themes. Reflecting on lived experience becomes a process of analyzing the thematic aspects of that experience. From a human science perspective, theme analysis does not consist of the application of predetermined categories to a text; grasping and formulating themes is not a rule-bound process, but neither is it arbitrary. Rather, it is a disciplined application of the concept of the hermeneutic circle: understanding of the whole arises from understanding of the parts (i.e., themes), but identification of the parts grows out of the emerging comprehension of the whole.

Gadamer's (1960/1992) description of the general process of interpretation can be used to clarify the process of thematic analysis. The relationship between the interpreter and the text is like that between speakers in a conversation. Just as in a conversation there is a dialogic process of questioning and answering, so in thematic analysis each emergent theme can be viewed as the answer to a question that the text puts to the reader—an answer that is then put into the conversation with the text and becomes the subject of further questions and answers.

The analysis of personal journals of later life is carried out through the selection and highlighting of statements in the journals that pertain to the experience of becoming an older person. Statements that relate to the same aspects of the overall experience of aging are grouped, and an attempt is made to express in writing the meaning of the selected group of phrases.

Interpretation

In terms of the strict practice of hermeneutic phenomenological reflection, the activities of close reading, the isolation of themes, and the crafting of texts articulating those themes constitute the activity of research. Put another way, the answer to the question "What does this text mean?" is given in the coherent articulation of its themes. Following this perspective, hermeneutic phenomenology becomes a science of examples. Evoking lived experience, not the confirming or disconfirming of universal laws, is the goal of research. Accordingly, articulations of the themes in the personal journals of later life, in and of themselves, can be understood as providing answers to the research question, "What is it like to be an older person?"

However, given that human science oriented gerontologists are historically situated in a scientific culture that has been engaged in systematic discourse about human development for about one hundred years, it is hard not to *interpret* the journals, in the sense of relating descriptions of aging found in the journals to gerontological concepts and theories. In fact, because any reading is necessarily carried out in the context of the reader's forestructures of understanding, clarification of the reader-researcher's response in terms of associations between themes in the text and prevailing gerontological thinking could be considered a necessary part of the overall human science research enterprise. The meaning of the text resides in its themes, but the meaning also resides in the text's connections with the larger discourse of gerontology. A single text clearly does not prove one or another theory, but it can be placed in an imaginary dialogue in which it is used to illustrate the theory or highlight aspects of the experience of aging not reflected in the theory.

A process that parallels the steps of description of themes followed by theory-based interpretation has been proposed by Spence (1989) in his critique of psychoanalytic case studies. Central to his argument is the theory-laden nature of what are ostensibly the objective facts that provide evidence in support of psychoanalytic theory. Patients' accounts of their experience are not given in their own words; they are filtered through the author's theoretical assumptions. Material included is preselected with the aim of making the best case. The clinical reports are carefully fashioned to persuade and could be more accurately construed as rhetorical exercises than as presentations of evidence.

Spence proposes that as a corrective a distinction be made between *etic* and *emic* data. Emic data are expressed in the categories and meanings of the subject. Etic data are expressed in the researcher's language or the categories of some theory. In the current practice of case study reporting, a significant portion of the data is cast in etic formulations. Spence is arguing for a revision of the genre of case study reporting in which a significant proportion of the data would be expressed in an emic manner, that is, in the patient's own words.

The reader would have access to concrete portions of the original observations and could better evaluate their translation into etic abstractions.

The etic/emic distinction was initially proposed by the linguist Kenneth Pike, who considered himself to be carrying forward the ideas of Edward Sapir. Pike (1967) viewed "etic" and "emic" as standpoints for the description of behavior— both linguistic and nonlinguistic—intending to convey by the word *standpoint* the idea that the terms constituted a convenient distinction, not a rigid dichotomy. According to Pike, the principal differences between the etic and emic standpoints could be summarized through a series of contrasts. Among these were the ideas that the etic approach was cross-cultural, with units of analysis available in advance, whereas the emic approach employed units determined during the analysis of a particular culture. The etic scheme of analysis is created by the investigator and imposed on the culture, whereas the emic scheme of analysis would more accurately be described as discovered, rather than created. Descriptions from the etic standpoint are, in a sense, alien to the culture, with criteria external to the culture under investigation, whereas emic descriptions provide an internal view, with criteria chosen from within the system. Measurement from an etic standpoint is absolute and direct; from an emic standpoint measurement is relative to the internal characteristics of the system.

Pike (1967) offers an analogy for understanding the etic/emic distinction in terms of alternative descriptions of a car. In an emic approach an analyst might describe the functioning of a particular car as a whole and might include charts showing parts of the whole car as they function in relation to one another. In an etic approach the analyst might describe the elements one at a time as they are found in an auto parts store, where bolts, screws, fan belts, and alternators from various models and makes of cars have been systematically filed according to general criteria.

The etic/emic distinction parallels that between the description of themes in personal journals and their interpretation in terms of gerontological theory. In isolating themes, the effort will be directed at staying close to the author's words. Subsequently, the isolated themes will be interpreted in light of developmental theory.

To summarize, the approach to the study of personal journals of later life used in this book consists of close reading of these texts, isolating and describing themes, and, finally, reflecting on those themes in light of developmental theories.

THE USE OF PERSONAL DOCUMENTS
BY PSYCHOLOGISTS

Use of the Term *Personal Document* in Psychology

"Personal documents may be defined as any self-revealing record that intentionally or unintentionally yields information regarding the structure, dynamics and functioning of an author's mental life" (Allport, 1942, p. xii). This definition, offered in Gordon W. Allport's brilliant monograph *The Use of Personal Documents in Psychological Science*, establishes the domain into which the consideration of personal journals of later life falls. By this definition, Allport intended to encompass all first-person, author-generated texts addressing "life as it is lived" (p. 56), a phrase he used to designate what he saw as an appropriate point of origin and constant touchstone for psychology.

Personal documents, so defined, may be deliberately devoted to self-scrutiny and self-description or may be only incidentally self-revealing. Included in Allport's definition are autobiographies, responses (in the form of written or verbatim transcripts) to open-ended questionnaires, diaries, collections of letters, and expressive and projective documents. Excluded from the definition are texts that also address the structure, dynamics, and functioning of mental life, but do so from the outside. Examples of documents Allport intended to exclude are third-person case documents such as biography, medical and institutional records, clinical accounts, and descriptive sketches.

The distinction between first-person documents and third-person documents seems initially to be straightforward, but on further consideration, the difference becomes blurred. Clearly, there are texts in which authors speak for themselves without a lurking researcher. Examples are autobiographies, letters, and diaries generated outside the context of research. Clearly, there also are texts that are about individuals but in which the voice of the individual is not heard. Examples are case reports, in which the account is purely that of the psychologist or social worker. But there is a substantial gray area in between. The form that epitomizes this gray area is the life history. Life histories can be viewed as autobiographies or as cases, as first-person or as third-person documents. They are written by a researcher, but typically, they attempt to give voice to the person whose life will be inscribed and who would otherwise not have a written life. Plummer (1983) has pointed out that it is best to think of personal documents, which he terms documents of life, as falling along a continuum ranging between accounts that are purely of the subject, that is, uncontaminated by the researcher, and accounts that are purely of the researcher, that is, uncontaminated by the subject. At the former end of the continuum would be, for example, original diaries; at the latter end would be, for example, case reports written entirely in the language of diagnostic categories and psychodynamic formulations. The two ends of this continuum could also be described by using the etic/emic distinction: the emic document contains the uncontaminated voice of the subject, and the etic document contains the uncontaminated voice of the researcher.

As Plummer notes, there is a point on this continuum where, on the one hand, the subject is more or less allowed to speak for himself or herself, but where, on the other hand, the researcher accumulates a series of themes, partly derived from the subject's account and partly derived from theory. Plummer terms this method systematic thematic analysis. It is characteristic of many life histories. But it is also the approach adopted in this book, in which the diaries are thematized, relying on the author's own words, and then interpreted.

The difficulty with the terminology, the problem of trying to sort out exactly what is or is not a personal document, has been enormously clarified by Norman Denzin. Denzin (1989a) observes that the major terms that surround and define the area he labels the biographical method spill over into each other. Terms like oral history, personal history, life history, autobiography, biography, self-story and personal experience narrative define *each other* and do so in terms of what Derrida (1967/1978) would call *différence.* "The attempt to give a fixed meaning to each term is doomed to failure. It represents a logocentric, scientific bias that must be overcome and displaced" (Denzin, 1989a, p. 47).

Be that as it may, in tracing the history of the use of personal documents in psychology, the emphasis here will be on consideration of research relating to preexisting personal documents. Thus, for purposes of the present discussion, the rich research on life histories will be excluded.

Allport's monograph (1942) traced the history of the use of personal documents (as he defined them) in psychology, the varying purposes to which they are put, special considerations related to each of type of document included in his definition, and the cases for and against research based on personal documents. The issues he raised, especially in terms of both the strengths and the limitations of the personal document approach, are just as pertinent today as when he articulated them fifty years ago. Any researchers working in this area will quickly find themselves grappling with the points raised by Allport either through their own reflections on their work or through critical appraisals by their colleagues. Two specific issues raised by Allport to be discussed later in this book are what I term the issues of analyzability and authenticity: What makes a particular journal analyzable in the sense of useful from a psychological perspective? How do we know that the text authentically represents the author's feelings? Allport's analyses of these issues still provide valuable bases for formulating responses to these important questions.

At this point in the introduction to the study of personal journals of later life, however, it will be useful to review Allport's history of the use of personal documents up until the time of his monograph and then to highlight the subsequent history of the use of personal documents in psychology down to the present.

The Early History

Allport points out that psychology was born in the nineteenth century using what were, in effect, personal documents. These documents took the form of psychologists'accounts of the functioning of their own minds. Helmholz's investigation of vision was based on his accounts of the functioning of his own eyes; Ebbinghaus based his theories largely on the operation of his own memory. This introspectionist approach predominated in early psychology. "It was assumed that the introspective deliverances of the philosopher-psychologist were necessarily infallible and that they were sufficient and typical for mankind at large" (Allport, 1942, pp. 3–4).

Toward the end of the nineteenth century, the pendulum swung abruptly away from dogmatic introspectionism and toward controlled experiments upon others. The shift was driven by the highly influential work of Wundt and the prestige of evolutionism, which directed attention outward toward other organisms.

Allport notes, however, that the initial expectations of the experimental age were that data obtained from studying others would demonstrate the same uniformity and typicality that had been obtained when individual researchers studied themselves. Such, of course, was not the case. Individual differences surfaced and in the final years of the century the concepts of variety, range, distribution, and clinical types came into favor. This opened the door for the use of case studies and personal documents.

The first great work of psychology to use personal documents was William James' *Varieties of Religious Experience* (James, 1901). James sought to put his empiricist ideas to the test by examining self-reported religious experiences (what Allport terms topical autobiographies) of religious people describing their most acutely religious moments. He did not follow early empiricist tradition of trying to identify a unitary religious experience, but rather elaborated *varieties* of religious experience. The method of using topical autobiographies was suited to the topic of the research. "No other method seemed available to him for discovering the fundamental ways of men coming to terms with the universe" (Allport, 1942, p. 7). Nothing has changed since James's time regarding the appropriateness of using personal documents, like diaries, to get at personal meanings and the ways people come to terms with the universe.

The early history of the use of personal documents also includes the work of G. Stanley Hall on adolescence (1904), which drew heavily on autobiographical writings, such as those by Goethe, George Sand, Helen Keller, and John Stuart Mill, and the work of Freud. Examples of the use of first person documents in Freud are his treatments of Goethe's *Dichtung und Wahrheit* (Freud, 1904), Jensen's novel *Gravida* (Freud, 1907), and Schreber's memoir of his mental illness (Freud, 1911). In reviewing the use to which Freud put personal documents Allport observes that, unlike James, Freud does not first present his cases and then draw his conclusions; rather, he uses the personal documents as exemplifications of theories previously formed. Allport, prefiguring

Spence's (1989) critique of psychoanalytic case reports, notes that his criticism of Freud's use of personal documents could be extended to the already (in 1942) very large literature of psychoanalytic cases in which each case seems forced into a preselected analytical mold.

The Twenties and Thirties

A pivotal event in the history of the use of personal documents for all the social sciences was the publication between 1918 and 1920 of Thomas and Znaniecki's *The Polish Peasant in Europe and America* (1958). In the 1920s and 1930s, this work was viewed in sociological circles as the finest exhibit of advanced sociological research and theoretical analysis. It has been termed a turning point (Allport, 1942, p. 18) and a milestone (Bruyn, 1966). Plummer (1983), who has written an appreciative assessment of the impact of this work, talks about how it provides a symbolic sociological birth of the line of thinking in sociology concerned with accurately linking the inner pursuit of self and the outer world. Thomas and Znaniecki's work initiated the heyday of the human document in sociology. Allport's treatment of the work (1942, pp. 18–22) indicates that it also played an important role in the debates of the psychology of the era about appropriate topics and methods of research.

The Polish Peasant was monumental in scope. It was originally issued in five volumes and contained more than 2200 pages. The work was prompted by the tremendous influx of Poles to the United States between 1899 and 1910. By 1914, Chicago had become the largest Polish center in the world after Warsaw and Lodz (Plummer, 1983). The study addressed questions about social organization, the impact of social change on community and family, abnormality, relations between the sexes, and social happiness. Of equal importance, however, was the methodological mission of the authors.

Thomas and Znaniecki distinguished between the objective factors of a situation and the subjective interpretation of that situation by social actors and advanced the position that both the objective and the subjective factors must always be taken into account in any social study.

Thomas and Znaniecki relied heavily, but not exclusively, on personal documents. One volume consists of the autobiography of Wladek Wisniewski, a Polish immigrant to Chicago. Another volume uses 764 separate letters arranged into 50 series.

Because of its broad impact on the social sciences, *The Polish Peasant* was selected by the Social Science Research Council (SSRC) as one of three works to be subject to an intensive critical appraisal in conjunction with the SSRC's mandate to improve the quality of research in the social sciences. The Council's study was written by Herbert Blumer and published in 1939 (Blumer, 1939). Blumer's study acknowledged the importance of *The Polish Peasant*, was sympathetic to the authors' philosophy and methods, but focused attention on the problems surrounding the use of personal documents. Consequently, the SSRC commissioned two further studies dealing exclusively with the use of personal documents. The first was Allport's, addressing the use of personal documents in psychology, and the second was prepared by Louis Gottschalk, Clyde Kluckhohn, and Robert C. Angell, who reviewed the use of personal documents in history, anthropology, and sociology (Gottschalk, Kluckhohn, & Angell, 1942).

In the years between the publication of *The Polish Peasant* (1918) and Allport's monograph (1942), there were important studies in psychology that relied on personal documents. Among these were those Buehler's investigations of "the curve of life," which used biographies (Buehler, 1935; Buehler & Massarik, 1968); Baldwin's studies of the structure of a single personality, which used a set of letters (Baldwin, 1940;

Baldwin, 1942); and Allport, Bruner, and Jandorf's study of personality under conditions of social catastrophe, which used autobiographies (Allport, Bruner, & Jandorf, 1941). Allport notes that at the time of his review, two to three hundred authors had employed personal documents in psychological research, but then goes on to comment that scarcely more than a dozen "seem to have given thought to the method they employ" (p. xv).

The Post–World War II Era

Allport's monograph makes a strong case for the use of personal documents. He shows how an epistemologically and methodologically enlightened use of such documents can enhance understanding, prediction, and control, which he saw as the aims of science. Although supporting the use of personal documents, he was scornful of their casual and uncritical use, decrying studies that were conceived loosely and executed in a pedestrian fashion.

However, Allport's advocacy of personal document research did little to alter the objectivist, behaviorist, and positivistic course of psychology in the postwar period. The ensuing years have seen very limited use of personal documents in psychological research. Writing in 1981, Wrightsman observed that it was regrettable that personal documents had been overlooked as sources of data about personality development (Wrightsman, 1981) and in 1988 he noted that the use of personal documents in psychology had not advanced much beyond that summarized by Allport in 1942 (Wrightsman, 1988).

There are some notable exceptions to the general absence of personal document research in contemporary psychology. Moreover, as will be described below, interest is increasing.

One of the most extensive analyses of personal documents in the post-World War II era was carried out by Allport himself and reported in the book *Letters from Jenny* (Allport, 1965). In the first part of this book Allport presents an edited version of 301 letters written to two young friends by Jenny Grove Masterson while she was between the ages of 58 and 70. Adhering to his own injunction to present the case first and do the conceptualizing later, he follows the presentation of the letters with analyses from three theoretical perspectives: an existential (phenomenological) approach, a depth (psychoanalytic) approach, and a structural, dynamic approach.

Personal documents also constituted the data for research by Rosenberg and Jones (1972) who analyzed the implicit personality theory in works of Theodore Dreiser and by Sears (1979), who analyzed the effects of childhood experiences of loss and subsequent separation anxiety in the letters and fiction of Mark Twain.

Several recent examples of personal document research are studies by Haviland and Kramer (1991) examining Anne Frank's diary for the relation between emotional expression and cognitive level; Abigail Stewart and associates (Peterson & Stewart, 1990; Steward, Franz, & Layton, 1988) analyzing the diaries and novels of Vera Brittain for the Eriksonian themes of identity, intimacy and generativity; and Espin, Stewart, and Gomez (1990) investigating a collection of letters written by an adolescent girl in terms of the interplay of normal developmental processes and traumatic life events.

It seems likely that we are entering a period of renewed interest in personal document research in psychology. The pendulum has swung yet again. We are now in the era of the interpretive turn in the social sciences (Geertz, 1980; Rabinow & Sullivan, 1979; Rabinow & Sullivan, 1987). In psychology, a narrative theory of identity, described in Chapter 8, has been elaborated (Cohler, 1982; Gergen & Gergen, 1983; Gergen & Gergen, 1988; Sarbin, 1986). Both these trends will undoubtedly lead to increased appreciation of personal documents— texts in which identities are inscribed, awaiting interpretation.

THE HUMAN SCIENCE TRADITION
IN GERONTOLOGY

Human science research focuses on elucidating lived experience. Over the years, without necessarily using the term *human science*, various gerontologists have argued for adopting approaches that allow for the possibility that older people themselves could more fully inform us about the experience of aging.

Foremost in this group is Bernice Neugarten. For example, in her 1973 essay on personality and aging for the American Psychological Association's volume of the state of the art of psychological perspectives on aging, Neugarten wrote

> [E]specially needed are investigations in which small samples of adults are studied in detail and in which attention is centered on intimate social networks and subtle aspects of interaction. . . . Studies that would be particularly valuable are those in which respondents are taught to give introspective accounts of the cognitive strategies they employ in dealing with inner and outer life events. (Neugarten, 1973, pp. 326–327)

Neugarten expanded on this idea in a 1985 essay in which she explicitly linked her ideas to the interpretive (i.e., hermeneutic) tradition (Neugarten, 1985). Of special relevance in the context of studying personal journals of later life is Neugarten's call in that essay for use of a broader array of methods in gerontological research, most notably autobiographical accounts.

Another gerontologist who, throughout his astonishingly productive career, has striven to expand the boundaries of what is considered admissible as data on aging is Robert Kastenbaum. Kastenbaum has been concerned with the lived reality of aging from his earliest work on subjective or "felt" age (Kastenbaum, 1964) to his most recent work on the experience of creativity in later life (Kastenbaum, 1992). In the same 1973 volume in which Neugarten's essay on personality and aging appeared, Kastenbaum was asked to contribute an epilogue (Kastenbaum, 1973). In this essay, he argued that no matter how formidable the methodological challenge, old people do have their inner lives and that we do not have a comprehensive gerontology unless we know something about this realm.

Another early advocate for a hermeneutic perspective in research on aging was Bertram Cohler. Beginning with his 1982 essay on personal narrative and the life course, Cohler has advocated adoption of the interpretive perspective (Cohler, 1982; Cohler & Galatzer-Levy, 1990). Drawing especially on Paul Ricoeur's philosophical contributions on narrative (Ricoeur, 1981, for example), Cohler argues for studying the manner in which people maintain a sense of meaning and coherence through time.

Working from a qualitative, symbolic interactionist perspective, Jaber Gubrium, beginning with his early works in the mid-1970s (Gubrium, 1975; Gubrium, 1976) and continuing through to his current writings (Gubrium, 1986; Gubrium, 1992), has conducted research that consistently turned to the meanings that older people themselves imparted to their situations.

A major event in the articulation of the human science perspective in gerontology occurred in 1988 with the publication *Qualitative Gerontology*, edited by Shulamit Reinharz and Graham Rowles (Reinharz & Rowles, 1988b). Like Gubrium, these researchers come out of sociological, rather than psychological, backgrounds, where the concerns of human science are conventionally addressed under the rubrics of interpretive social science (Rabinow & Sullivan, 1979; Rabinow & Sullivan, 1987) and qualitative sociology (Schwartz & Jacobs, 1979). Far more significant than the label, however, is what Reinharz and Rowles identified as the central concerns of qualitative gerontology:

> . . . describing patterns of behavior and processes of interaction, as well as revealing the meanings, values, and intentionalities that pervade elderly people's experience or the experience of others in relation to old age. . . . A primary focus is on understanding and conveying experience in "lived" form with as little *a priori* structuring as possible. Qualitative gerontology attempts to tap the *meaning* of experienced reality by presenting analyses based on empirically and theoretically grounded descriptions. (Reinharz & Rowles, 1988a, p. 6, emphasis in original)

The gerontological work which, to this point, most explicitly links the study of aging with the human science tradition, is the book edited by Eugene Thomas, *Research on Adulthood and Aging: The Human Science Approach* (Thomas, 1989). The studies collected in this volume all address the process of meaning-making in later life. The methods vary widely and include analysis of textual material, participant observation, intensive case studies, and semistructured interviews. In each of the chapters, the authors have sought to understand the world by relying on the eyes of their informants rather than by testing hypotheses generated from other sources and imposed on the data.

The human science perspective on aging is also linked to the work that has been conducted over the past 20 years on the humanities and aging (Cole & Gadow, 1986; Cole et al., 1992; Moody, 1988; Polisar, Wygant, Cole, & Perdomo, 1988; Spicker, Woodward, & Van Tassel, 1978; Yahnke & Eastman, 1990). There is an affinity between human science and the humanities because of human science's recognition of the cultural embeddedness of experience, including the experience of aging. Representations of aging in literature and art derive from their creators' culturally-rooted experiences. Those representations, in turn, help shape others' experiences of aging.

This book emerges from my deep respect for the writing (and speaking) of those gerontologists who in the past have urged the adoption of a human science perspective on aging and is intended to serve as another step in the continuing development of that perspective. Because of the data being used—published personal journals—this book also lies precisely at the intersection of human science and the humanities and should illuminate the interrelationship between cultural images found in literature and the study of human development.

Diaries, Journals, and Personal Journals   2

The mere intention to use published diaries and journals as sources of information about the experience of aging opens up a wide range of questions pertaining to the form itself. Among these questions are the following: What is a journal or diary and is there a difference between them? What are the origins of this literary form and in what ways is it connected to larger cultural trends? What are the similarities and differences between diaries and journals and other forms of nonfiction, such as memoirs, autobiographies, and letters? Whose diaries and journals are published? How have diaries been viewed by literary critics? It would be arrogant to engage in a gerontologically minded analysis of diaries without first addressing these issues.

TERMINOLOGY

In English we sometimes use the word *diary* and sometimes use the word *journal* to designate a literary form built around daily—or, at least, periodic—entries. What is the difference?

Are diaries more superficial or more profound than journals? Are diaries more factual and journals more reflective?

Fothergill (1974), Mallon (1984), and Nussbaum (1988), critics whose work on diaries as a form of literature are most helpful, agree that there is no consistently applied distinction in the way the terms are used. It is true that some published texts labeled *diaries* are mere records of daily events with little reflection on the meaning of those events. In this category are diaries such as that of the colonial farmer William Byrd, whose diary is a mechanical record of his daily activities. Even his sexual conduct is turned into a dull regimen of "committing uncleanness," "rogering," and "polluting myself." However, other published texts labeled diaries, such as those of Anne Frank and Virginia Woolf, are full of personal reflection. Similarly, the term *journal* may be applied to books that concentrate on the objective reporting of events, such as the journals of Lewis and Clark, but may also be applied to books whose focus is on self reflection, such as the intimate journal of George Sand. Mallon argues that the terms are hopelessly muddled and they might as well be used interchangeably. He points out that we can go back to Dr. Johnson's *Dictionary* and find him making the two terms more or less equal. To Johnson a diary was "an account of the transactions, accidents and observations of every day; a journal" (Mallon, 1984, p. 1). Mallon suggests that if synonymity was good enough for Johnson, we ought to let it be good enough for us.

Although no consistent distinction can be made between journals and diaries, it is possible to distinguish between journals and diaries in which the life of the author is the prime subject and works in which the author is principally reporting on external events, such as those describing travels, chronicling political affairs, or keeping diary records of special interests like gardening or fishing. The former, which, following Fothergill (1974), we will designate as *personal journals* or *personal diaries*, are examined in this book.

HISTORICAL PERSPECTIVE

The diary is a form of creative expression with a long history. The last four books of Augustine's *Confessions*, dating from the fourth century, provide a very early example of diary-like writing. The famous books on English diaries by Ponsonby (1922; 1927) and Matthews (1950) discuss texts that are cast in recognizable diary form from as early as the fifteenth century. The modern usages of the words journal and diary begin to appear in the sixteenth century (Nussbaum, 1988). The seventeenth century, however, marked the diary's proliferation.

Between the fifteenth and the seventeenth centuries, four categories of prediary texts can be identified (Fothergill, 1974). These categories are significant, because the diary form that evolved from them bore the mark of these early texts. The first of the prediary forms is the travel journal. Francis Bacon described the importance of keeping such a journal in one of his essays written in the early years of the seventeenth century. The idea was to make a young man's tour of the continent more worthwhile. The journal was to be used as an instrument for seeing more clearly and remembering more profitably. The second diary precursor is designated the public journal. This category covers a range of works that have in common the fact that their writing was performed for the sake of public usefulness. It includes transactions of public bodies, ships' log-books, and annals of military campaigns, but it extends to self-appointed chroniclers, who feel compelled to compile the annals of their age. Much contemporary diary writing continues in this vein. The third of the prediary types is the journal of conscience, consisting of works whose purpose is self-examination in moral terms with particular emphasis on the workings of sin and repentance and the evidence of God's dealings with the soul. This type of writing was prescribed as part of a regimen of self-development by Puritans, Quakers, and other dissenting groups. There are detailed published guidelines dating from the mid-seventeenth century for keeping such journals. Fothergill notes that the availability of such guidelines means that if you undertook to keep such a journal of conscience you "would begin with already formed ideas of how to go about it, what sort of thing to include, what tone to adopt . . ." (p. 17). The structure of this type of diary was given and that structure imposed a formalized rhetoric and narrow subject matter. The existence of a well-known form of daily inscription has obvious relevance for the later development of the diary. The fourth prediary category is the journal of personal memoranda. This type encompasses works which are accumulations of jottings, notes of the day's events, records of business transactions, and so on.

These four early forms of journaling, as some would call it today, serve as points of reference for later diaries. Moreover, Fothergill (1974) argues that no major diary draws its impetus from only one of these sources and that great diaries draw on all four.

The landmark diary of the seventeenth century was that of Samuel Pepys. Pepys' diary was written between 1660 and 1669, when Pepys was between 27 and 36 years old. There are entries for every day of this period except for 11 days in the fall of 1668. The diary, which was not published until 1825, has been described as condemning all previous diary-keeping to the prehistory of the genre (Fothergill, 1974). It is praised for its close observation, flexibility of language, picturesque passages, exceeding frankness (Latham, 1983) and the balance it achieves in subject matter and in attention to both the outer and inner life (Fothergill, 1974).

Just as Pepys's diary serves as a milestone in the history of the diary in the seventeenth century, Boswell's diaries serve as milestones of diary writing in the eighteenth century. Covering the years 1762 to 1778, Boswell's diaries are marked by a perpetual oscillation in the author's self-concept. Boswell is torn between two images of himself: one as a man of character and self-control who will conform to the dictates of right behavior, the other as a person of striking originality and exuberance, ready for anything, obligated only to realize his unique qualities.

By the beginning of the nineteenth century, diary writing began to be recognized as a literary activity open to both established and nonestablished writers. The writing in diaries came to be characterized by immediacy, self-reflection, and an effort toward authenticity. In romantic British diaries of the early nineteenth century, such as the 3,000-page diary of the artist Haydon, and in nineteenth century French diaries known as *journaux intimes*, these qualities were carried to an extreme. The writers of *journaux intimes* demonstrated their cultivated capacity for passionate responses to music and literature and their unusual sensitivity to all kinds of stimuli (Fothergill, 1974). A further aspect of the evolution of the personal journal in the nineteenth century was the adoption of the personal journal form as a presentational strategy for fiction (Abbott, 1984), an approach that continues to be used by contemporary authors (Updike, 1975, for example).

In the Victorian era, diary writing as a conventional habit among persons of culture reached a peak. Victorian diaries, written by travelers, soldiers, politicians, and clergymen, present enormously detailed pictures of contemporary life, attitudes and values, but tend to have little autobiographical energy or individual accent, probably out of a sense of the necessity of maintaining proper decorum. In this country, a different type of nineteenth-century diary has been the subject of recent attention. The substantial body of diary writing by pioneer women has created considerable interest among feminist literary critics. Schlissel (1982) provides a good introduction to this literature, highlighting the way that the diaries document the dramatic details of these women's everyday existence.

Two trends in twentieth-century diary-writing are notable and are evidenced in the published diaries considered in this book. The first is the preparation of a diary with the intention to have it published immediately. We have many published journals from earlier centuries; however, the publication of such journals is typically attributable to someone other than the author and almost always someone from a later historical period. It was not until the twentieth century that writing a journal with the avowed intention of publication came about. Barbellion's (1984) journal covering the years 1903–1917 represents an early example. Barbellion, a biologist and aspiring writer who struggled with poor health, sought to redeem his life through his diary, which he fully intended to have published. All of the five older diarists considered in this book were well-known authors who had already produced poetry, fiction, or essays. The diaries of four of the five were written with the understanding they would be published.

The second twentieth-century trend is the tendency of diarists to use psychological concepts and sometimes even to make explicit reference to psychological theorists such as Freud, Jung, and Erikson in their self-reflections. An example of this trend is the use made by Anais Nin, in her voluminous diaries, of the ideas of Rank and Jung. Among the diarists considered in the present book, Scott-Maxwell and Sarton, in particular, draw on their familiarity with psychoanalytic theorists in reflecting on their own lives.

It is worth noting, too, that in the twentieth century we have seen the growth of the journal as a vehicle for self-understanding, self-guidance, and expanded creativity for students and the psychologically minded public. This trend is apparent in the numerous published guides to journal writing (Baldwin, 1991; Progoff, 1975; Rainer, 1978), the workshops and classes on journaling available around the country, and the use of learning journals as an approach to student evaluation.

The overall development of diary writing as a literary form, thus, can be summarized as that of movement from diary writing as a by-product of other activity to diary writing as crucible of consciousness and as a literary end in itself.

DIARIES, AUTOBIOGRAPHIES, MEMOIRS, AND LETTERS

One way to characterize the personal diary or journal is that it is writing both of oneself and by oneself. Because other types of writing can be similarly characterized, it is instructive to think about the relations among these forms.

Autobiography is another literary form in which one writes of oneself and by oneself. Three characteristics of autobiographies are worth noting in order to clarify their relationship with diaries. First, in its contemporary form, autobiography involves an attempt to create a *coherent* narrative of a life. It is in the nature of narratives to explain. Narratives cannot help telling how things are and why they are that way (Trilling, 1972, p. 135) and autobiographical narratives are not exceptions. In autobiographies, people account for their actions and explain their lives. Events are selected to accommodate the demands of the narrative (Freeman, 1993).

Second, the author of an autobiography writes from the perspective of a completed sequence of events. At the time of their writing, authors of autobiographies (and often the readers) know what happened. The outcome is known, and the significant antecedent events—the ones worth telling—are those that are thought to bear on that outcome.

Finally, in autobiographies, the "I" that is writing thinks back to and writes about an "I" of an earlier time. The actor being described in autobiography is not identical to the actor doing the writing. The passage of time and the accompanying developmental changes create this differentiation of author and subject.

In contrast, in the usual conception of diaries, there is no coherent narration of a life. There are often inconsistencies and contradictions in a diary, mirroring the contradictions and uncertainties of daily life. As will be discussed below, the lack of coherent narrative in diaries has sometimes been the basis for denigration of their literary merit.

Unlike autobiographies, diaries are not written from the perspective of a completed series of events. Neither the author nor the reader knows how events will turn out. This actually creates a kind of dramatic tension in diaries that cannot be matched in autobiography. The authors' and readers' joint ignorance of the outcome of events adds greatly to the power of several of the journals considered in this book, most notably Grumbach's *Coming into the End Zone* and Sarton's *Endgame* and *Encore*.

Finally, for entries that deal with current events in the authors' lives, the "I" that is writing the journal is the same "I" that engaged in the events being recounted. There is no differentiation between author and subject occasioned by developmental change.

These distinctions between diaries and autobiographies are not absolute. Both diaries and autobiography are forms of nonfiction writing centering on recollection (Moffett, 1985). In the former, the elapsed time between the events and the writing is usually hours, days, or weeks, whereas in the latter the interval is more likely to be years. However, as the autobiographer's story approaches the present the gap in time between events and their inscription may approach that of a diary.

Additionally, although the entries in diaries tend to focus on events of the day or of the very recent past, those events may serve as the occasion for recollecting and recounting events of the more remote past. In fact, the interplay of past and present in the diaries under consideration in this book is one thing that makes them such valuable documents. They illustrate the way that moment-to-moment experience is suffused with the residue of events of the past. In each of the diaries of later life considered in subsequent chapters, the authors reflect back, in the manner of an autobiography, on events of the remote past in order to account for an action or a feeling of the present.

Another type of text related to the diary and autobiography is the memoir. Like autobiographies and personal journals, memoirs are concerned with the recording of experience. In both memoirs and autobiographies, the experiences written about tend to be separated from the act of writing by years, rather than by hours or days as would be the case with journals. Like autobiographies, memoirs are written from the perspective of a completed series of events; the outcomes are known. But whereas the aim of autobiography is to provide an account of the author's life, memoirs tend to be concerned with persons other than the author or events to which the author was a witness. The focus is typically outward. What the narrative in memoirs explains is not primarily the author's life but external events and persons.

There are varying degrees of "being outside" in memoirs. The author may be a participant in events or merely an observer or eyewitness. But what makes the memoir form an example of the personal document is that the events documented in memoirs share the quality of having "happened to" the writer.

Among the writers considered in this book, May Sarton is unique in that she has written in both the journal and the memoir form. Her journals recount her day-to-day experience. In the journals, neither the writer nor the reader knows how the story will turn out. Sarton's memoirs, *I Knew a Phoenix* and *Plant Dreaming Deep*, are written after the events have transpired. In *Plant Dreaming Deep*, for example, she recollects striking off on her own at age 40 and settling into an old house in a small New Hampshire town. The events described in *Plant Dreaming Deep* occurred over an eight year period. In *I Knew a Phoenix*, she recalls her encounters with people who were influential in shaping her life. The focus is on their lives rather than hers. Although both of these books are autobiographical, in the sense that they describe aspects of Sarton's life, neither one is, strictly speaking, autobiography. They lack the comprehensiveness that we associate with autobiography and are better viewed as memoirs.

In addition to diaries, autobiography, and memoirs, a fourth type of personal document with potential relevance for illuminating aspects of the experience of aging is the letter or exchange of letters. Letter writers may use their correspondence to reflect upon their day-to-day experiences much as a diarist would. When a set of such letters exists it may serve much the same function as any of the diaries considered in this book.

Although letters are written for a specific audience, a particular other, and diaries are not, the ideal of audience or other is not completely absent from diary writing. After analyzing over 150 published journals, Mallon (1984) asserts that although the diarist's "you" may not be palpable; there is typically an *implied* "you" in diaries. Dinnage (1984, November 8, p. 3) observed that "there is no diary writer including ourselves and Uncle Henry who never imagines the other person reading the page."

Interestingly, diary entries sometimes take on the character of letters. The epistolary nature of diaries is, of course, most clearly revealed in the convention many young diary writers follow of beginning their entries with the salutation "Dear Diary." Additionally, of course, in diaries intended for publication, the writer knows from the outset that others will be reading the entries, just as is the case with letters. Such diaries could be viewed as a form of one-sided correspondence.

Autobiographies, diaries, memoirs, and letters all narrate personal experience. Although it is possible to distinguish among them, each of these forms spills over into the other. Autobiography approaches diary as the time narrated draws close to the present. Diary approaches autobiography to the extent that the entries weave the past into the present. Memoir approaches autobiography as it becomes more comprehensive and centered on the self. Diary approaches letter as the audience becomes more specific as in diaries intended for publication.

We should not be overly concerned with assigning a text to

one or another of these categories. These types of texts define each other in terms of difference. Particular instances may be quite justifiably assigned to more than one form. Ultimately, all these forms of personal experience narratives may prove useful in their own ways for illuminating the experience of aging.

DIARIES AND THE IDEA OF THE INDIVIDUAL

The rise of the personal journal is linked to a broad trend in Western culture known as individualism. It is as if the theme of our era is captured by Polonius's admonition to Hamlet: "This above all, to thine own self be true." The origins of individualism have been variously traced to the Renaissance, to the seventeenth century, and to the eighteenth century, but there is general agreement that it emerged in full force with the Romantic movement of the early nineteenth century (Trilling, 1972; Weintraub, 1978). Individualism posits the centrality and sovereignty of the individual (Shotter & Gergen, 1989, p. 9). It involves a conception of the person as a "bounded, unique, more or less integrated motivational and cognitive universe, a dynamic center of awareness, emotion, judgment and action, organized into a distinctive whole" (Geertz, 1979, p. 229). The central point here is to understand that the person, so described, is a sociohistorical and sociocultural product, not a naturally occurring object. The contemporary Western ideal of individualism is not the only possible view of the self. On the contrary, it is a rather peculiar idea within the context of the world's cultures and even within the context of Western history. Gagnon (1992) argued, for example, that at the end of the Enlightenment

> the vast majority of people, including most of the urban intelligentsia, experienced their individuality as being constituted by a limited and seemingly coherent bundle of socially given

roles that changed only slowly during the course of their lives. . . . By the end of the eighteenth century and the beginning of the nineteenth century . . . an increasing number of people began to experience the relationships that they had with others, what we would now call "the roles that they were required to play," as detached from or alien to who they "truly" were or who they wanted to be. Thus a private protoself was being detached from public roles. (p. 222)

The nineteenth century Romantics furthered the shift from the public to the private self, claiming that their conduct, which violated social expectations, was justified by the presence of a unique and private source of meaning, their vision. Development of the vision often involved a journey away from the demands of collective constraint. During these travels there would be a crisis of estrangement, and in the triumph over this crisis would be found a confirmation of the existence of a self that was transcendent over the prescribed roles of social life. The Romantic belief in the possession of a private self that was the ultimate seat of authority for connecting meaning and action was disseminated as a potential form of mental life to larger and larger audiences during the course of the nineteenth century (Gagnon, 1992). Because people increasingly saw themselves as unique individuals, it was natural to engage in a form of expression to record that uniqueness.

DIARIES AS LITERATURE

Despite the publication of many diaries from the beginning of the nineteenth century to present, the diary has not been viewed as a form of writing worthy of serious attention until relatively recently. In terms of their critical appraisal, diaries, as a form of autobiographical writing, shared the devalued status of formal autobiography. However, although formal autobiography came to be recognized during the 1950s, 1960s, and 1970s as a respectable literary genre in works of literary criticism such as those by Pascal, Olney, and Morris, diaries tended to be viewed as inferior or failed versions of the "real thing." Nussbaum cites an example of the early critical stance toward diaries from Donald Stauffer's 1930 book about English biography:

> The diary makes no attempt to see life steadily and see it whole. It is focused on the immediate present, and finds that the happenings of twenty-four hours are sufficient unto the day. It becomes, therefore, not the record of a life but the journal of an existence, made up of a monotonous series of short and similar entries. Furthermore . . . the diary has scant claim to consideration, for it makes no pretense to artistic structure. (Stauffer, 1930, p. 55)

A similar point is made in a very influential essay on autobiography by Georges Gusdorf (1980):

> The author of a private journal, noting his impressions and mental states from day to day, fixes the portrait of his daily reality without any concern for continuity. Autobiography, on the other hand, requires a man to take a distance with regard to himself in order to reconstitute himself in the focus of his special unity and identity across time. (p. 35)

The fundamental weakness of diaries, then, as reflected in these quotations, is lack of unity, discontinuity, absence of a cohesive self, and lack of artistic structure.

Contemporary movement of thought, however, has created the occasion for a re-evaluation of the literary status of diaries. Specifically, as Nussbaum (1988) has pointed out, in the postmodern theoretical context we begin to relinquish demands for theme, pattern, structure, and certain meaning. Benstock (1988) has argued that the diary form has no investment in creating a cohesive self over time. The diary form

exploits difference and change over sameness. Diaries do not
attempt to cover over "internal cracks, disjunctions, rifts, and
ruptures," nor do they presuppose a stable "I" from which the
unitary perspective on the life is offered (Benstock, 1988, p. 19).

Moreover, among contemporary feminist critics, the very
demand that autobiographical writing present (in Gusdorf's
phrase) "a special unity and identity across time" has come
to be viewed as a distinctly masculine perspective on the representation of self. Citing the work of Chodorow, Dinnerstein,
and Miller, Smith (1987) has argued that women experience
themselves in relatively "interpersonal, subjective, and immediate ways" (p. 13). The demand for unity and identity in
autobiographical writing may run counter to women's ways
of knowing themselves. The devaluing of discontinuous narratives of self may stem from an "androcentric paradigm of
selfhood."

Smith's description of the inappropriate application of androcentric criteria to texts produced by women (including many
women's diaries) is analogous to the arguments presented by
Gilligan (1982) about the masculine bias in the early work
on moral reasoning. Using Kohlberg's schema for evaluating
moral reasoning, girls and women receive, on average, lower
ratings than boys and men. As Gilligan has demonstrated,
this differential is not due to a deficiency in the development
of women's ability to reason about moral issues, but rather
is attributable to a difference in moral voice, a tendency for
girls and women to emphasize equity as a basis for moral
judgments versus a tendency in boys and men to emphasize
equality. The original coding scheme for stages of moral reasoning was biased toward the masculine moral voice and thus
resulted in lower average scores for girls and women. Similarly, until recently the literary response to autobiographical
writing has been weighted toward the masculine form of self-
representation, emphasizing coherence and unity and result-
ing in a devaluing of more feminine forms of self-presentation,
which emphasize fluctuation and discontinuity.

In sum, one argument from recent critical thinking about diaries is that rather than being measured against formal autobiography, the diary should be evaluated in its own right for the aspects of experience it uniquely has to offer.

How shall we characterize the aspects of experience offered by the diary genre? Fothergill (1974) has succinctly expressed the key elements uniquely captured in diary form. Despite the many variations within the form, what diaries have in common is that they are written in the first person as a discontinuous series of more-or-less self-contained responses to the writer's present situation and recent experience. The diary format has the capacity to fixate subjective experience in a way that approximates the actual passage of the future into the past.

An additional point raised from the perspective of recent critical evaluation of diaries is the importance of distinguishing between the person who writes the diary and that person's projection into the published work. Writing of two British diarists, Fothergill warns us that a statement like "Ryder is inhibited by constant anxiety, whereas Kilvert gives himself to his emotions" refers not to the law student and the clergyman but to the characters who live on the pages of an eighteenth century and a nineteenth century book. This point has also been made effectively by Spacks (1976), who, commenting on all forms of autobiographical writing, notes that real people asserting their identities in prose create themselves through acts of imagination. Autobiographical writing should not be viewed as factual truth, but rather as a way of wrestling with truth.

The logical extension of this position is that diarists should be accorded the status of characters of fiction. Whereas characters in actual fiction exist as the objects of someone else's imagination, the heroes and heroines of autobiographical writing achieve identity as the objects of their own imagination. The mechanism for creation of character in fiction is, typically, the *invention* of events and description of the characters' responses; the mechanism for creation of character in diaries and other autobiographical writing is the *selection* of events and description of the writer's (i.e., the character's) responses (Spacks, 1976).

The view that the characters that emerge in the pages of published autobiographies and diaries are, in a sense, fictional, is not alien to contemporary thought in the social sciences. Those working on life histories and interpretive biography are well aware of the way that the accounts they provide are images of subjects' lived experiences in particular historical moments, not the lives themselves. Both fiction and autobiography are narrative arrangements of *facts* (events that are believed to have occurred) and *facticities* (how those facts were lived and experienced by interacting individuals) (Denzin, 1989a, p. 23).

However, in some work in the social sciences, the fictional quality of subjects' self-presentations is obscured by the impress of methodology. Thus, in doing interviews or administering questionnaires, one can easily forget that what is obtained from respondents, no matter how rigorous the methodology, is a characterization of experience within culturally available (and socially acceptable) conventions of expression.

To say that diaries should be appreciated as a distinct form of autobiographical writing rather than as a failed form of formal autobiography does not answer the question of what constitutes, from a literary perspective, a good diary.

In some of the early critical work on diaries (Matthews, 1950; Ponsonby, 1922), it was argued that the defining characteristic of a good diary is unpremeditated spontaneity and sincerity. The underlying notion was that the hallmark of the good—or the "true"—diary is that it is written with effortless frankness in a process akin to unselfconscious talking to oneself. The implication is that endeavoring to write well, considering the formal structure of the book one is writing, addressing oneself to a putative reader, thinking of publication, or editing one's entries would be viewed as a corruption of the required spontaneity of utterance and as introducing a falseness and even an ethical flaw into the text. Artifice, to use Spacks's (1976) term, was viewed as contrary to the essence of the diary form.

The criterion of unpremeditated spontaneity and sincerity derived, in part, from what had been the prevailing view of Pepys's diary. Pepys was held up as the quintessential diarist (Ponsonby, 1922). It was assumed that every night for nine years, he just scribbled down what had caught his attention at the moment. In the early 1970s, this image underwent considerable revision (Pepys, 1970–1973). Examination of the manuscript of the diary made it clear that the entries had not all been made daily, but adhered to the convention of seeming so. They were not freehand improvisations, but rather were composed from notes and rough drafts and entered with painstaking neatness. As Fothergill (1974) notes, it is ironic that Pepys was not nearly as Pepysian as had been believed.

The heart of the problem with using unpremeditated sincerity as a criterion for evaluating the literary merit of a diary is the idea that sincerity and premeditated utterance are opposed to one another. Fothergill (1974), writing of diaries, and Spacks (1976), writing of formal autobiography, both argue that there is no conflict between deliberately employing literary techniques and strategies, such as striving for effects, using literary embellishments, even editing the entries, and the literary merits of a diary. Spacks points to the difficulty, sometimes approaching a sense of desperation, in trying accurately to convey in words what we are like, what we have experienced. She writes that the capacity of autobiographical writers to achieve an image that can even partially express themselves depends finally on their literary artistry and their mastery of the *techniques* of evocation (p. 311, emphasis added).

Therefore, the mere presence of conscious stylistic devices in a diary, or the fact that the entries were edited, should not disqualify it from consideration as a good or great instance of the form. To the contrary, great diaries will be carefully crafted and will exhibit the same literary modes of expression found in great fiction. Nonetheless, we are still left with the question of what does distinguish the best examples of the genre, aside from the fact that they are well-written.

Fothergill (1974) proposes two criteria. The first he terms *the book of the self*, the second the book's *imprint*. The term *book of the self* is intended to designate the sense that emerges in some diaries that, unwittingly, a book has been emerging whose character and conventions have been established and whose final form is the shape of the author's life. In diaries that exhibit the characteristic of being books of the self the diarist writes of being committed to the book, rather than to the mere exercise of diary writing. In such diaries, the writer will be likely to make overt reference to the diary as "this book," taking care over it, worrying about bringing it up to date, and perhaps expressing the idea that abandoning the diary project would be tantamount to failing to complete a book. The diary, in effect, becomes conscious of itself. The diary itself seems to foster an awareness of the patterns and processes at work in the life of the writer; the writer comes to appreciate the shape his or her own image and likeness have taken.

Imprint, Fothergill's second criterion, refers to the range of reflection present in the diary entries. Regardless of whether a diarist is deliberately or unwittingly composing a book of the self, it is possible to ask how wide a range of the person's life would be found in a random sample of entries. To satisfy the imprint criterion requires that a rich composite of reflections be present in the journal, including both descriptions of the external world and the vicissitudes of feeling. The extent to which a diary combines these elements is an important measure of its achievement. "A diary consisting of nothing but cogitation and self-analysis presents as distorted an imprint as one which only describes things seen and done" (Fothergill, 1974, p. 57).

Virginia Woolf's frequently quoted description of the art of diary, in the entry for April 20, 1919, effectively captures what it means for a diary to have a broad imprint and also to be a book of the self:

> Moreover there looms ahead of me the shadow of some kind of form which a diary might attain to. I might in the course of time learn what it is that one can make of this loose drifting material of life; finding another use for it than the one I put it to, so much more consciously and scrupulously, in fiction. What sort of diary should I like mine to be? Something loose knit and yet not slovenly, so elastic that it will embrace anything, solemn, slight or beautiful that comes into my mind. I should like it to resemble some deep old desk, or capacious hold-all, in which one flings a mass of odds and ends without looking them through. I should like to come back, after a year or two, and find that the collection had sorted and refined itself and coalesced, as such deposits so mysteriously do, into a mould, transparent enough to reflect the light of our life, and yet steady, tranquil compounds with the aloofness of a work of art. The main requisite, I think on re-reading my old volumes, is not to play the part of censor, but to write as the mood comes of anything whatever; since I was curious to find how I went for things put in haphazard, and found the significance to lie where I never saw it at the time. (Woolf, 1953, p. 13)

In writing about the diary as a "capacious hold-all" and of writing "as the mood comes of anything whatever," Woolf is arguing for a broad imprint, a great variety of topics. When Woolf says entries have "coalesced into a mould," she is alluding to the sense of the self that emerges in retrospect, the patterns that were present though unperceived but which, having been perceived, may themselves enter into subsequent diary entries.

What relevance do these criteria for the literary merits of diaries have for the use of diaries by gerontologists to illuminate the experience of aging?

Quantitative research typically treats all responses as being "on a par." An individual subject's response in a reaction time experiment is just as valuable as another individual's response in the same experimental condition in terms of computing the mean score for subjects in that experimental group and, thereby, generating a statistical description of what it is like to be a member of that group on the dimension of interest. In this sense, quantitative research is eminently egalitarian.

In contrast, research on descriptions of the experience of aging found in personal journals is not so egalitarian. Not all people have the capacity to express themselves equally well in language. The data provided in the journals of different individuals may not be equally valuable, as would be the case in quantitative research. Fothergill's criteria provide a reasonable start at characterizing standards that could be used by gerontologists to evaluate the potential merits of a diary of later life for investigating the lived experience of aging. To the ideas of book of the self and imprint should be added the ideas of thick description and insight.

The ideal personal journal from the perspective of investigating the experience of aging is one that does more than just record what a person is doing, even if it also alludes to accompanying feelings. Rather, many of its entries should be of the sort that anthropologists (Geertz, 1973) and sociologists (Denzin, 1989b) term "thick description," that is, entries that present detail, context, emotion and the web of social relationships that join persons to one another.

Additionally, insight, a term from psychoanalysis (Moore & Fine, 1990), is also a characteristic of the ideal personal journal from the point of view of research on the psychology of aging. Is the writer capable of seeing herself as others see her whether or not she agrees with the public verdict (Allport, 1942, p. 132)? Does the writer present analyses of the dynamic factors contributing to his conflicts? Are there flashes of recognition leading to cognitive and affective reorganization and a sense of emotional freedom? The best journals for understanding the experience of aging would exhibit these qualities.

There is an interesting parallel here with the psychoanalytic idea of analyzability. In the practice of psychoanalysis it is recognized that not all people who seek psychoanalysis are analyzable. Originally, the determination of analyzability was based on age and diagnostic categories. Only individuals under the age of fifty and suffering from transference neuroses (hysteria, phobia, and obsessive-compulsive disorder) were deemed acceptable. As the practice of psychoanalysis evolved, the scope of indications for analysis widened (Wiersma, 1992). Some of the features currently used to assess analyzability are sufficient self-object differentiation to achieve a stable transference, an ability to free associate, sufficient resources to make the necessary sacrifices of time and money, the ability to tolerate frustration and to tolerate anxiety without fleeing the situation. Contraindications include inadequate reality testing with magical thinking and the use of primitive defenses such as projection and denial; excessive tendencies toward self-mutilation or destruction; and sadistic or criminal behavior (Moore & Fine, 1990).

The fact that not all patients are suitable for analysis does not, in itself, invalidate either the practice of psychoanalysis or the descriptions of human behavior that emerge from that practice. Similarly, the idea that only certain personal journals of later life are suitable for analysis does not invalidate either the practice of journal analysis or the descriptions of aging that emerge from it.

WRITERS, TEXTS, READERS

The personal journals considered in this book were all written by professional writers. Grumbach, Sarton, and Vining had each published works in various genres prior to the publication of their diaries, including children's books, novels, poetry, memoirs, and biographies. Olmstead was an editorial writer for a daily newspaper and had also written an account of his experiences in World War II. Scott-Maxwell had written plays, a memoir, and several works on relationships between men and women. Obviously, the fact that these diarists were recognized writers had a great deal to do with the publication of their diaries. An author's familiarity with the world of publishing and track record of prior publications are major factors in determining whether or not a book is published. There is no reason to think that there are not unpublished diaries as deserving of publication as those treated here but written by authors who are not familiar with the world of publishing and who have no prior publications. Even if the authors of such diaries (or their heirs) wished to have them published, the chances of finding publishers willing to invest in such books are slim. Therefore, to use published diaries of later life as sources of information about the experience of aging implies heavy reliance on the work of professional writers.

There is a temptation to view the diaries of writers as being somehow less true or authentic than the diaries of ordinary people. This thought is predicated on the notion that being a writer somehow removes one from the class known as people. Obviously, writers are people. What distinguishes them is their skill at casting experiences into language, not the experiences themselves.

Because of professional writers' skill at expressing themselves in words, the probability that their diaries will, in terms of the criteria discussed above, be good from a literary or research perspective is greater than for the diaries of nonprofessional writers. However, the assessment of a diary's literary quality or usefulness for research on aging does not depend on the credentials of the writer, but rather on the work itself. Moreover, several of the great English diaries reviewed by Fothergill, most notably that of Pepys, were written by people who published no other works.

As is the case with many diaries, the authors of the diaries considered here are explicit about their reasons for inscribing their day-to-day experiences. For example, Vining writes that she wants to record "the things I do for the last time or enjoy less keenly" (Vining, 1978, p. 5). Such rescuing of experience from annihilation is a common motive of diary writers (Fothergill, 1974), one to which Pepys makes explicit reference.

At the end of *Journal of a Solitude*, Sarton states her purpose in keeping the journal:

> This journal began a year ago with depression, with much self-questioning about my dangerous and destructive angers, with the hope that self-examination would help me to change. (Sarton, 1973b, pp. 206–207)

Sarton is alluding to the use of journals for self-improvement. In citing this reason for keeping a journal, Sarton is harking back to the Puritan journals of conscience, some of the earliest examples of the journal form.

Elsewhere in *Journal of a Solitude*, she makes a simple comment that applies generally to reasons why established writers keep journals. She writes, "My business is the analysis of feelings" (p. 44). For Sarton and presumably for other established writers the analysis of feeling can take a variety of forms: poetry, fiction, or journal writing.

Established writers also keep journals to refresh themselves. In a review of the Woolf diaries, Dinnage (1984, November 8, p. 3) comments that "the diary is the spontaneous overflow of a committed writer's tremendous energy." Speaking of Woolf, Dinnage remarks that "as she breathed she wrote." The diaries served to liberate, freshen, and uncramp Woolf. Journals may serve for writers as muscle stretches do for athletes: as a means of preparing for the main event or of recovering from the sustained expenditure of imaginative effort.

From comments in the diaries, it is apparent that the authors were, in addition, motivated by some of the same factors that motivate other diarists (Fothergill, 1974). Included would be the prospect of future pleasure at the recollection of pleasant events, leaving a legacy for the edification of others, the exercise of sociological interest in recording observations of cultural practices, and fending off loneliness.

In considering the diaries of frail older people, such as Scott-Maxwell's diary and the later diaries of Sarton, an additional function of the diary becomes prominent. As Spacks (1976) has noted in connection with autobiographical writing in general, to tell a story of oneself is an affirmation of power even when the story contains emphatic defects. When frail older people set down a personal interpretation of personal experience, they are, in effect, declaring their autonomy and demonstrating the dominance of mental life despite the physical losses they have endured.

In this chapter we have considered the personal journal as a type of literature. As we begin the consideration of particular journals in the following chapters we should bear in mind that these works arose out of a literary tradition with a long history and that the authors of the books we will be considering drew on that shared tradition in selecting incidents and expressing what, for them, were experiences that were their own. Moreover, the works we are considering emerge out of a culture that posits the centrality of the individual. The form itself, in which these authors have chosen to express themselves, is congruent with the individualistic bent of our culture. We look to these works not because we presume they are "representative" of the lives of older people, but because they provide insightful, well-written descriptions of what can happen in later life by people skilled in the analysis of feeling.

The ensuing five chapters will adhere to the approach to

the study of personal journals described in Chapter 1, in which the idea of isolating and describing themes and, then, providing interpretations was put forward. In each chapter, there is first a profile of the author. This will be followed by a section describing themes in the journal. Finally, in a commentary section, interpretations will be offered in terms of ideas from developmental psychology and gerontology.

Elizabeth Vining and the Transition to Later Adulthood

3

Being Seventy: The Measure of a Year, by Elizabeth Gray Vining (1978), presents a remarkably clear picture of a healthy, successful woman during the year of her seventieth birthday. As we read Vining's book, we are aided in seeing the world as she does because she is an experienced writer with a highly developed capacity for reflective musing on the events of her day-to-day life.

PROFILE

Elizabeth Gray Vining was born in Philadelphia in 1902, the younger of two daughters. She was a graduate of Bryn Mawr College and the Drexel Institute of Library Science (later Drexel Institute of Technology) and in her twenties worked as a librarian in Chapel Hill and New York, while also beginning her career as an author, initially of children's books (under the name Elizabeth Janet Gray) and later of adult biography and fiction. Vining married at age 26 and four years later was widowed when her much-loved husband died in a

car accident in which Vining was also seriously injured. She
never remarried. After the accident, Vining found spiritual
comfort in the community of Quakers in Philadelphia and became involved with a variety of Quaker activities including the
American Friends Service Committee. In 1946, she received the
extraordinary honor of being appointed tutor to Crown Prince
Akihito of Japan. This experience profoundly affected her life
and led to lifelong friendships with the Japanese royal family
and a degree of fame she had not previously received. She later
wrote *Windows for the Crown Prince*, which was widely read,
recounting her experiences serving as a royal tutor.

During the 1920s, 1930s, and 1940s Vining's reputation
as an author of children's books steadily increased. In 1943,
she received a Newbery medal for one of her children's books,
Adam of the Road, published in 1942. In her journal, she
records that she took great pride in the fact that almost all of
her children's books stayed in print for many years. When she
wrote *Being Seventy*, she had completed 23 books including
novels, biographies, and her autobiography, *Quiet Pilgrimage*
(Vining, 1970). She was living in an apartment in Philadelphia and was in reasonably good health. She had no immediate family, her older sister having died three years earlier.

THE JOURNAL

The format of *Being Seventy* adheres to the general conception of what a journal should be like. There are entries on 143
different days between August 26, 1972, and October 5, 1973,
the day before Vining's seventy-first birthday. Each entry
indicates day and date. When Vining has traveled and arrived
at a new place, location is also shown in the heading. The
entries vary in length, with some as short as one hundred
words and others extending to two to three pages. The content of the entries also varies. The jumping off points may be

visits with friends, letters received in the mail, her reading, or simply an event of her day.

The most striking impression from the journal is how busy this woman is: She travels; she spends one month in Japan participating in a writer's conference, another month at a writer's colony on Ossabaw Island off the coast of South Carolina, and two months on annual summer vacation in New Hampshire. She lectures: she mentions giving seven different speeches and presentations during the year, but it is not clear that all her talks are mentioned in the journal. She entertains: she hosts extended visits of friends from Japan and from Ireland. She is actively involved with friends: she visits friends, writes to friends, talks to friends. And she drives: up and down the East Coast. All the while she is diligently working on a biography of Whittier, which she completes, types into final copy, and mails off to the publisher ahead of a September 1 deadline.

Clearly, this woman is highly engaged in the world. She has many connections to other people that occupy her time and attention; she has her work: her writing, which she calls the "basis of her life" (p. 83), "the soil out of which other things spring" (p. 128); she has a passionate interest in the events of the world in that momentous year, a year that saw both the bombing of Cambodia and the Watergate hearings.

Two interlocking themes are especially prominent in the journal: first, a heightened awareness of age and, second, a sense of culmination and impending change.

Awareness of Age

Vining is conscious of being old. She is aware of her age as a factor in social interaction and as a cause of behavior. The journal is particularly useful in clarifying the varying contexts in which self-consciousness about age may emerge in the day-to-day life of an older person.

> I wish I could stop thinking about being old. It's not that I mind it so much or fear it; it's just that I am so aware of it all the time. (p. 3)

What she means by "all the time" is elucidated in several other entries. It is not that at every waking moment she thinks "I am old." On the contrary, "days go by when I scarcely think of it" (p. 133). It is more that the fact of her age enters into consciousness with what she feels is great and, generally, unwanted frequency: "In how many different ways this business of growing old comes at one!" (p. 133).

Sometimes the fact of her age enters into consciousness as an explanation for mishaps or failings.

> I stumble on the stairs and think, "Old and clumsy. I suppose I'll get worse." A name or a word eludes my mind, and I think, "Losing my memory. . . ." (p. 3)

On other occasions the fact of her age enters into consciousness as the shocking recognition that she is labeling or has labeled as old a person who is her present age.

> I was eight, I think. I was playing with my friend Elizabeth Hutchinson, and we went in to see her grandparents, who lived next door in a large stone house. They both seemed to me incredibly old, he with his white beard and she with her black silk dress. I suppose actually they were no older in 1910 than I am now. (p. 7)

> As I look forward to Kendal . . . I sometimes catch myself thinking of all the nice things I am going to do for those old people there, and then I remember that I am one of those old people myself. (p. 187)

The most disconcerting example of the dissonance created by the recognition she is now in age and appearance what she used to view disparagingly as old comes with the discovery of a journal she kept when she was 31. She was surrounded then by four women in their 70s, approximately Vining's present age. At that time, she wrote:

> I am sorry for old ladies. Failing faculties and failing looks must be a constant irritation to unfailing vanity. . . . One pities them, one loves and cherishes them, one can so rarely like them. (p. 136)

She has moments of age awareness when talking to younger people. Toward the beginning of her stay at Ossabaw Island, she remarks that she is older than anyone else in the group and is unsure whether what she had to say will be interesting to the younger people. After spending several more weeks there, those concerns have diminished, but she comments that she still thinks of age from time to time. "I recognize that I am now out of the mainstream, and I am content" (p. 117).

In a paradoxical way, social interaction with people her own age can also have the effect of bringing age to consciousness:

> I am enjoying a luncheon party with lively conversation and laughter, and suddenly the thought comes, "Four widows over sixty-five having a good time as if they were young. How absurd" (p. 3).

Not unexpectedly, awareness of age comes to her when she reflects on her and her friends' age-related physical problems. Although Vining is apparently quite healthy and seems to have no limitation on an ability to engage in extensive driving and air travel, in the journal she does mention several age-related physical problems, her declining vision, forgetfulness, and arthritis. Also, Vining mentions friends of her generation whose age-related impairments are far more severe than hers and who, in several cases, have had to move to long-term care facilities.

Vining's age consciousness is also heightened on the anniversaries of birthdays of friends and relatives who have died. At a younger age, these birthdays would have been celebrated with gifts or birthday meals at restaurants. Now, these occasions can only be marked with an entry in the journal.

Part of what makes these moments of age awareness so shocking to Vining is the sense that she doesn't feel old, so how *could* she be the age she *knows* she is? She writes:

It isn't as if I felt old. I don't. Inside I feel often as gauche, as shy, as incapable of wise or effective action as I did at sixteen, or as surprised and delighted by unexpected beauty. (p. 4)

Thus, she cannot help being aware of her age, being aware that she is now the age that she used to think of as old and that other people now think of as old. Yet, this awareness is coupled with what she senses as a contradictory awareness, the awareness that she doesn't feel old.

Culmination and Change

The daily obbligato of messages about being old is linked to a second major theme in this journal, the idea of culmination and impending change. She writes:

A door shuts. It is shut not in one's face but behind one. In front is a new landscape, bleak perhaps at times, lit no doubt at others by mysterious beauty, but cut off in the distance by a wall, which for the first time is close enough to be visible. One stands in a limited space, with the door behind and the wall somewhere in front. (pp. 4–5)

The sense of culmination can be seen in her reactions to attending her fiftieth college reunion:

I shall not attend any more. . . . It was a good reunion, perhaps the best we have had, and for that reason it is well to end on it. Later we shall be putting a brave face on age; now we are enjoying its rewards. From now on we live *sub specie aeterni-tatis*. We have made our contribution, whatever it is; we are on the threshold of a great change, whatever it may be. (p. 141)

Aging, itself, inevitably leads to changes, but in Vining's case, the sense of an impending momentous change that runs through the journal pertains to the decision she is weighing about relocating to a retirement community. The journal tracks the unfolding of the decision to make this major alteration in her life.

When the reader first joins her on August 26, 1972, about a month before her seventieth birthday, the decision-making process is well underway. She has already made a deposit on an apartment at Kendal, a Quaker retirement community under construction in Chester County, outside Philadelphia. However, this decision has not yet really been made. She is at the brink. She is not yet fully committed to the move and can still recover her deposit. During the year, Vining exposes her internal debate over the move. The debate centers on self-definition. She has had many moves in her adult life, and at one point notes that she typically lives at most six to seven years in the same place. A move to a retirement community, however, would be quite different. In all likelihood, it would be a final move and one that would unequivocally define her as an older person. The move would, in effect, publicly mark her transition to later life.

An entry on November 11 captures Vining's reservations and hesitancy about the move to the retirement community. She was coming home on a train from downtown Philadelphia and met a friend, whose husband had recently died.

We talked about getting old. . . . Not wanting to live alone in the country, she moved to an apartment in Philadelphia. She has friends at Folkways [another retirement community], but says she could not live there because she could not stand going into the dining room every day and seeing all those old women. (p. 28)

Vining comments:

Well, there it is. That is the crux of the matter, the depressing part of a retirement community, even the best of them: the segregation of the aged. That and the finality of it. Once in, will one feel trapped? (pp. 28–29)

Although the issue of age segregation is important for her, especially in view of her many younger friends, the consequences of the move in terms of self-definition seem to be equally distressing. "I shall be one of them [older people] if I go in. I shall be as depressing to them as they to me" (p. 29).

However, external circumstances must be weighed along with the internal considerations in making a decision such as the one she is facing. She asserts that people approach "what is so mincingly called the Later Years" in two ways: with the "stick-it-out-in-the-world policy and the duck-into-safety policy." She recognizes that the first policy sounds more gallant but realizes that what looks like the gallant course may not be wise in her circumstances.

If you have family, sons and daughters or devoted nieces and nephews, to step in and take responsibility if you fall in the bathroom and break your hip, then you can afford to live dangerously. If you are, as I am, entirely alone, I think you at least examine carefully the second alternative. (p. 29)

In an entry written six weeks later, she reveals that the idea of moving to Kendal has taken on more definiteness. Commenting on Christmas presents, she writes:

More and more I welcome the consumable: food, calendars, soap, wine. With Kendal ahead I have to reduce my possessions, not add to them. (p. 78)

A month later she visits Kendal and sees a friend who has moved into a sample apartment. After a luncheon there, she comments that "Kendal looks like a good thing" (p. 88).

In February and March of 1973, Vining lived and worked at a writer's colony on Ossabaw Island, off the coast of North Carolina. Being surrounded by younger writers invigorated her and revived the internal debate over the move to Kendal. On March 15, she writes:

> How much would it depress me to be surrounded by aging and dying people? How much would the pressure of the commu- nity bother me? (p. 117)

An entry in mid-May reveals her continuing ambivalence. She remarks that she is "going through files and posses- sions, weeding out in case I should move next fall" (p. 135). The words "in case" indicate that a firm decision has not been made, but the action of weeding out reveals more cer- tainty about the move than she admits to herself or to her journal.

In an entry on May 24 she acknowledges that she has in- deed reached the decision to make the move.

> Exactly when did I decide to go to Kendal when it opens? The day that I paid my first substantial deposit—which is still re- vocable—or the day I wrote in my diary "Kendal looks like a good thing?" (p. 142)

At the end of the summer she curtailed her vacation in order to make final arrangements for entering Kendal. In an entry on August 20 she comments:

> Just when I made the final decision I am not quite sure, but here I am. Up to now I have known that I could withdraw at will and so was not committed. Now I shall be; to be exact, the day after tomorrow I shall be. (p. 176)

The entry two days later compellingly expresses Vining's sense that she has passed through the threshold she described at the beginning of the journal and entered into a new phase of her life. Following delivery of a payment that constituted the final commitment to the move, she writes:

> A momentous step has been taken, and I poke myself gently to see how I feel, as one touches with a tentative tongue a tooth that might be going to give trouble. (p. 177)

She comments that, apart from all the fuss of moving, she is extremely satisfied and grateful she is going to Kendal. In this entry she again considers the disadvantage of being surrounded by old people in the age segregated retirement community. The resolution of this problem that she gives herself and the reader seems to be informed by the professional discourse of gerontology that had begun to penetrate the popular media.

> As to everybody's being old there, they will, most of them, be young old, enjoying the first exhilaration of retirement. There is a difference between the young old and the old old. But that stage, too, will come, of course. (p. 178)

The last entry is written the day before her seventy-first birthday. In it, she reflects on the good news that her manuscript for the biography of Whittier has been accepted and in the process underscores her sense of having made the transition to being old.

> What an advantage the old have—in some ways—over the young! Five weeks ago I sent off the manuscript of my Whittier book. . . . Once I would have been in an agony of suspense. . . . Now in these weeks I have given it a passing thought from time to time, quite prepared for it not to be what was wanted, since I am in many ways out of step with the present writing world. Today a letter comes . . . saying that I have done a "splen-

did job" and I shall be hearing from the copy editor soon. . . .
I am very much pleased, but—and doubtless this is the other
side of the coin—not wildly elated as I once would have been.
Still, the letter is a *very* nice birthday present. (p. 194, emphasis
in original)

COMMENTARY

Levinson's Conception of Adult Development

The sense of being on the brink of a major change in life is
certainly not restricted to older people. It can occur in earlier
adult years and can be associated with a variety of events not
necessarily tightly linked to chronological age—falling in love,
starting graduate school, getting a new job, and being preg-
nant. However, the sense of being on the brink, the sense of
culmination and impending change described by Vining, bears
a striking resemblance to two earlier periods in people's lives
that are age-linked. These are the transitions from adolescence to young adulthood and from young adulthood to
middle age.

Our understanding of this feeling of being on the brink of a
major life change, particularly as it relates to people around
age 20 and around age 40, has been enhanced greatly by
Daniel Levinson's idea of the development of the individual
life structure (Levinson, Darrow, Klein, Levinson, & McKee,
1978; Levinson, 1986). Levinson and his colleagues conducted
intensive biographical interviews with 40 men between the
ages of 35 and 45. The purpose of the interviews was not only
to obtain the facts of the men's lives, but also, and more im-
portantly, to help the men recall the circumstances surrounding the choices they had made in their lives and what
their decisions had meant to them. Such an approach yields
a welter of details pertaining to particular choices made in
particular lives. Out of this welter of detail, however, Levinson

was able to organize the information about the lives, compare one life to another, and discern regularity by means of the concept of life structure.

The life structure is a person's set of attachments at a given time and the priorities among them. In this context, the term *attachment* is intended as a broad term covering that conceptual territory occupied by other terms such as *relationship, engagement, connection* and *cathexis*. Typically, the life structure consists of attachments in the domains of family, occupation, leisure roles, and religious activities, but can also include attachments to a house, a community, or a geographic area. Understanding a life structure consists of understanding the meaning of attachments in a person's life. For example, two men may have very similar demographic profiles consisting of being married, having two children, being employed at about the same level in the same company. But the life structures of the men may differ greatly, with one having the job at the center of his life and the family as a peripheral attachment, while the other is centrally invested in family with the job relatively peripheral.

The meanings and relative importance of the set of attachments that constitute the life structure at a given moment are revealed most sharply when people are forced to choose between attachments. An example of such a forced choice might be having to decide to accept or refuse a better job in another part of the country. For some people, geographic locale is a highly significant component of the life structure. Taking a job in another part of the country is simply out of the question. The geographic locale in which they reside is central to their sense of self and the good life. For others, it is self evident that career comes first. The idea of refusing or not seeking a job in another part of the country would seem foolish. Choosing to refuse a better job because it would take one away from a preferred geographic locale reveals one ordering of the components of the life structure. Accepting the job, despite the necessity for geographic relocation, reveals a different ordering. It is the history of such choices that Levinson puts at the center of his investigations into the life course; he considers such choices pivotal in the analysis of the evolution of the life structure.

Levinson sees the individual life structure undergoing change throughout life, but he found that change in individual life structure is neither uniform nor random. Rather, Levinson sees change occurring in bursts. Based on his research with the 40 men, his subsequent research on women (Levinson, 1986) and drawing on others' research on the adult life course, on biographies, and on literary texts, he presents a model of the adult life that proposes that individuals pass through stable structure-building periods succeeded by unstable, transitional, structure-changing periods. Structure-building periods, which typically last five to seven years, are phases of development in which people make certain key choices and pursue their goals within the framework for living created by those choices. Structure-changing periods, which typically last for five years, are those in which an existing life structure is reappraised, alternative possibilities are explored, and movement is made toward choices that form the basis for the life structure in the ensuing period. As a consequence of the length of the structure-changing periods and their repeated appearance during the course of adult life, almost half of adulthood is spent in developmental transition. Questioning, reappraisal, and change are seen as normal and expectable, not as aberrant aspects of adult development.

The progression of structure-building and structure-changing periods is set in a larger framework of what Levinson refers to as eras. The four eras—Childhood, Early Adulthood, Middle Adulthood, and Later Adulthood—and the cross-era transitional periods represent the overarching organization, what Levinson calls the macrostructure, of the life course. Each era, according to Levinson, represents a distinct phase in biological, psychological, and social development.

Although all transitional, structure-changing periods carry

with them the sense of being on the brink of great change, those transition periods which bridge eras, the major units of life, are likely to be accompanied by a more intense experience of culmination and impending change than intermediate transition periods. "The move from one era to the next is neither simple nor brief. It requires a basic change in the fabric of one's life" (Levinson et al., 1978, p. 19). Vining's diary can, in Levinson's terms, be viewed as a description of the experience of passing through the last cross-era transition, the bridge between middle age and later adulthood.

Levinson's Model: Critique and Reinterpretation

Critical responses to Levinson's research and theorizing typically focus on his proposal that there is an age-linked developmental pattern to adulthood. The age-linkage is represented in his chart of the developmental periods, which shows a stair-step progression from stable period to transitional period to stable period and so on. Each period is linked to a particular range of ages, so that, for example, the period called Culminating Life Structure for Early Adulthood (earlier called Settling Down) is shown occurring between the ages of 33 and 40. Levinson has noted that often the critique of his finding of age-linked developmental periods takes the form of plain incredulity. It is averred that it is simply not possible that development should occur in so orderly a sequence during adulthood. Critics point to the way social roles and careers evolve in accord with highly variable institutionally defined timetables; given this variation how could there be an ordered pattern to adult development? Critics also point out the tremendous variation in the timing of major life events, what Neugarten has called the flexibility of the life-course, and the way that adaptation to such arbitrarily timed life events is undoubtedly a major force in shaping adult life (Neugarten & Hagestad, 1976). As Gergen (1980) has argued, for any individual the life course seems fundamentally open; human developmental trajectories may be virtually infinite in their variation.

Levinson has responded to these critics (1978; 1980; 1981; 1986) by reiterating and emphasizing that the pattern of age-linked developmental progression becomes visible through the lens afforded by the concept of the life structure. Single aspects of development, such as a particular biological change or specific life events (e.g., marriage or graduation from college) may occur at widely differing ages. Levinson asserts, however, that the idea of age-linked developmental change becomes apparent when, rather than examining single dimensions or events, the shape of a person's total life (the life structure) at a given moment is examined and followed over time.

How compatible is Levinson's conception of adult development with the human science perspective described in Chapter 1 (and which emerged as a clearly articulated position in psychology subsequent to Levinson's presentations of his ideas in the late 1970s and early 1980s)? There are two seeming incompatibilities between Levinson's model and the human science position. The first is that Levinson's conception of adult development, with its identification of the ages at which period transitions are expected to occur, seems to imply an automatic unfolding of the organism with relatively little active involvement of the organism itself. Clearly, any such idea of automatic unfolding runs counter to the premise that human beings are active makers of the meanings that give direction to their lives.

A second concern from a hermeneutic perspective is that Levinson's conception of adult development (especially as reflected in the chart of adult developmental stages) seems to posit a universalistic model independent of time or place that gives insufficient weight to the impact of language, culture, and history on shaping the life course. It could be argued that what Levinson is presenting is not *the* pattern of adult development, but rather a linguistically, culturally, and historically bound story, relevant only to the Western culture of our time.

In response to the first concern, it is important to note that although Levinson himself does not explicitly write from a human science perspective, he places great importance on the process of actively constructing meaning. The life structure, he reminds us repeatedly, is not a simple tallying of roles. "We have to consider the meanings and functions of each choice within the individual life structure" (1978, p. 43). From Levinson's perspective, part of what we are forced to take into consideration when we make significant life choices is our temporality, our aging, our progress through the biologically, psychologically and socially constituted eras of life. The life structure is not fixed once and for all at any point in the adult life course, because as long as we are alive we age. Aging creates instabilities in the life structure. Previously made choices take on new and, often, less satisfactory meanings with the passage of time. Moreover, all life choices are embedded in a temporal context. They are suffused with our awareness of our progress through the eras of development and our sense of always being poised between a presently remembered past and an anticipated future. The central place of temporality in human meaning-making is highlighted in the hermeneutic philosophy of Heidegger (Faulconer & Williams, 1985) but emerges as an empirical finding in Levinson's work.

The hermeneutic concern about the role of language, culture and history in shaping the life course is also addressed by Levinson. He acknowledges that the pattern of development he elucidated is contingent on the nature of human society at this phase of its evolution. The life structure is seen as the interface between the person and the sociocultural world (Levinson et al., 1978, Chapter 3) and is, necessarily, a product of that world. However, Levinson also stresses that we are biological creatures and that the progression of life structure changes is, in part, a response to biological givens. In this respect, Levinson is a *developmental* human scientist. Meaning-making is inextricably linked to cultural *and* biological givens. Human beings are not totally free to invent themselves, as seems to be asserted by what Mahoney (1991) terms the radical constructivists (Gergen, 1980; Watzlawick, 1984). We are embodied meaning-makers and those bodies age.

In view of this interpretation of Levinson's model, Vining's journal can be understood as tracking the reappraisal of a life structure whose meanings had become increasingly tenuous through the passage of time. The journal reveals the stresses placed on her existing life structure (and the positioning of self in the world that it entailed) by biological factors (her body), social factors (interactions with others), and psychological factors (temporal awareness). It also reveals her efforts to construct a new understanding of self in the world and to make choices based on that new understanding.

The Last Cross-Era Transition

As depicted in Vining's journal, the experience of making the cross-era transition into later adulthood consists, in part, of daily reminders that one is becoming old. These reminders arrive through bodily changes in oneself and one's friends, social interactions in which a person finds herself to be the oldest one present, the memory of past age categorizations of others. Also as described in this journal, the experience of passing through the last cross-era transition carries with it an intense sense of ending and culmination based on the knowledge and associated feeling that certain heretofore repeated events are occurring for the last time, be they last reunions, last trips, or a last relocation.

A vast professional and popular literature documents the first cross-era transition, the attempts of adolescents to build a first adult life-structure. This literature captures the accompanying feelings of culmination and new beginning. The fictional form that tells the story of coming of age is so common that, in German, a single word, *Bildungsroman*, designates this literature. The cross-era transition of mid-life has also been discussed in both professional and popular literature (Sheehy, 1976). Although it presents a general view of development over the course of life, Levinson's book itself deals mainly with the mid-life transition: men in the age range 35–45 years.

Thus, we are moderately well-acquainted with the era-bridging transitions between childhood and early adulthood and between early adulthood and middle adulthood. What it feels like to *become* an older person, to take steps such as that taken by Vining in moving to a retirement community, is relatively unknown. From this perspective, Vining's journal is a rare and valuable document. It is a rich description of the psychological landscape of the third cross-era transition, the transition between middle adulthood and later life.

May Sarton and the Tensions of Attachment

4

One must believe that private dilemmas are, if deeply examined, universal, and so, if expressed, have a human value beyond the private. . . . (Sarton, 1973b, p. 60)

No contemporary author has made a greater contribution to the genre of personal journals of later life than May Sarton. Her six published journals, which span 20 years of her life from ages 59 to 79, constitute an invaluable gift to those interested in studying the lived worlds of older people. Each book is important in its own right, but, for those interested in development in the later years, the principal value of these books lies in being able to consider them jointly and in so doing to trace the rise and fall of developmental problems over the entire period they cover.

PROFILE

May Sarton was born in Belgium in 1912 and came with her parents to the United States in 1916 to escape the war. She was educated in Cambridge, Massachusetts, and in Belgium at schools that emphasized the pleasure and excitement of study, love of poetry, and the dignity of the inquiring mind. For three years, she was part of the Civic Repertory Company in New York and for another three years directed her own theater group. This group failed when Sarton was 24, at which time she committed herself to a life of writing poetry and novels. A useful summary of her childhood and youth appears in Sibley's early biography (1972).

The 35 years between Sarton's initial commitment to a life of writing and the events recorded in the first of the journals of her later years were marked by immense productivity, the emergence of a loyal following of admirers, but limited critical recognition. During those years she published 10 books of poetry, 11 novels, and 3 stories for children. In the late 1930s and the 1940s, she traveled widely, lecturing at many American colleges and universities, and wrote book reviews and articles on theater and poetry. In addition to continuing to lecture, during the next two decades, she taught composition and creative writing on short term appointments at Harvard, Bryn Mawr, Wellesley, and Lindenwood College. She received numerous awards and grants, including a Guggenheim fellowship and Danforth and Phi Beta Kappa visiting scholar lectureships.

The publication of *As We Are Now* (1973a) brought Sarton to the attention of people concerned with the problems of aging in the United States. This polemical novel is about the struggles of a 76-year-old woman who has been forced to enter an inferior nursing home. It highlights the physical and emotional abuse to which many nursing-home residents may be subject and ends with an act of defiance by the heroine.

To understand the events that led to the publication of in the first of the seven published journals, *Journal of a Solitude* (1973b), it is helpful to be familiar with two previous works, *Plant Dreaming Deep* (Sarton, 1968) and *Kinds of Love* (Sarton, 1970).

Plant Dreaming Deep, a memoir of Sarton's move from Cambridge to Nelson, New Hampshire, describes the life she created in that rural community. The move was precipitated by the deaths of both of her parents, her mother in 1950 when

Sarton was 38 and her father six years later. She had remained quite involved with her parents through her 30s. They helped her financially, and she viewed their home in Cambridge as her home, although she actually lived in an apartment she shared with her long-time friend, Judith Matlack. Within a week of her father's death "the house had been sold, and within two months dismantled, the books gone, everything torn apart of the fabric of my parents' lives together" (Sarton, 1968, p. 22). At age 46, as a single woman and "orphan," Sarton decided to buy a house for the first time. Her choice was not to remain in Cambridge but rather to move into a dilapidated eighteenth-century farmhouse in the Monadnock Mountains of New Hampshire. In *Plant Dreaming Deep*, written eight years after this move, she recounts the difficulties of getting established in the house, bringing order to the grounds, and becoming accepted in the town; she describes her deep feeling for the people who came into her life; and she conveys the texture of her life, which is that of a person who is committed to work but who is also a great lover of people and of nature. Much of the content of *Plant Dreaming Deep* resembles that of the journals, which followed it over the succeeding two decades. It addresses, as the journals do, the themes of solitude, friendship, the beauty and power of the natural world, and the struggle to create both her self and her work. As noted above, however, its narrative style sets it apart from the journals. It is a memoir, rather than a journal. It does not recount events as they unfold but rather sets forth an organized distillation of eight years' experiences. Moreover, this particular memoir has a logical form. The descriptions move out in widening circles to encompass house, garden, neighbors, and community. It concludes with a characterization of her self in this place. Also, there is a dramatic structure to the narrative of the fall and subsequent rise in her fortunes over the eight years which makes the work resemble a novel. Viewed in this way, *Plant Dreaming Deep* tells the story of a woman who took on the challenge of establishing a solitary life in a remote place, who endured considerable difficulty, who learned much from the natural beauty of rural New England and from the strength of character of its inhabitants, but whose life also had deep roots in other places and in a past not shared by her neighbors.

Her next work, *Kinds of Love*, was Sarton's most complex and ambitious novel to that point. Set in Willard, a small New Hampshire town modeled on Nelson and drawing heavily on the people she encountered there, the novel is about what happens when an older couple who are long-time summer residents resolve to stay through the winter months. Portrayals of many kinds of love are woven into the story: love between old friends, between a husband and wife late in life, between a mother and an emotionally disturbed adult son; love of nature; the love of young lovers; and the love of people for their community. The novel also deals with courage in facing the ordinary adversities of poverty, illness, and old age. As Bakerman (1982) has noted, a central theme of this novel is the crucial importance of the life-long work of creating a self: "What is interesting after all is the making of a self, an act of creation, like any other, that does imply a certain amount of conscious work" (Sarton, 1970, p. 32).

Both these works are linked to *Journal of a Solitude*. In *Journal of a Solitude*, Sarton wrote that *Plant Dreaming Deep* presented a false view of the kind of person she was, that it presented her as a "wise old party" (p. 142) and failed to convey "the anguish of her life," particularly her "rages" (p. 12) and her "destructive angers" (p. 206). One of Sarton's aims in *Journal of a Solitude* was to present a more authentic version of herself than she believed was presented in *Plant Dreaming Deep*.

In *Journal of a Solitude*, Sarton also reflects on *Kinds of Love* or, more precisely, on the critical reception to *Kinds of Love*, particularly the review in *The New York Times*, which was devastating: "This novel, flawed in style and flabby in content, is filled with characters but does not bring the reader in to share the depth of their experiences" (cited in Blouin, 1978, p. 134). Although there were some favorable reviews, the *Times* review was emotionally bruising and financially harmful. In *Journal of a Solitude*, Sarton deals with the aftermath of this event. *Journal of a Solitude* seemed to establish for Sarton the possibility of the published journal as a form of creative expression that would complement her poetry and novels. It is a form which she has pursued in six subsequent works.

The period from the publication of *Journal of a Solitude* to the present has been marked by continued productivity and increasing public and critical recognition (Hunting, 1982; Hunting, 1986). In addition to the journals, those decades saw the publication of five books of poetry, five novels, two books of juvenile fiction, an additional memoir, and a collection of Sarton's criticism. Sarton's work became the object of sustained critical attention; her life and work have been the subject of two films. Most significantly, Sarton has come to be viewed as a woman who has given voice to struggles faced by many women, particularly women artists, and who has persevered in combating debilitating stereotypes—including stereotypes about aging and about sexual preference—until she finally achieved her place as an important and respected contemporary American writer.

THE JOURNALS

Sarton's journals present day-to-day experience during more than two decades later life. Each journal was published separately and can be read independently. Also, the journals are discontinuous. There are periods during the 22 years spanned by the seven books that are not discussed. During those periods Sarton was engaged in creative work which required her to set aside journal writing. Table 4-1 is provided in order to clarify the time periods covered in the five books and Sarton's age during those periods.

Table 4-1 Chronology of Sarton's Journals

Journal title	Year of publication	Journal dates	Sarton's age
Journal of a Solitude	1973	9/15/70–9/30/71	58–59
The House by the Sea	1977	11/13/74–8/17/76	62–64
Recovering: A Journal	1980	12/28/78–11/30/79	66–67
At Seventy: A Journal	1984	5/3/82–5/2/83	70
After The Stroke: A Journal	1988	4/9/86–2/21/87	73–74
Endgame: A Journal of the Seventy-ninth Year	1992	5/3/90–5/3/91	78–79
Encore	1993	5/5/91–6/24/92	79–80

The substantial period of time that is covered by the seven journals means that there are necessarily differences among them in content. The issues that predominated in Sarton's life at 59, such as the lack of appreciation of her work by literary critics and the breaking up of love relationships, differ from the issues she faced at 70, such as dealing with the consequences of success and adulation. And, not unexpectedly, with increasing age, Sarton came to face health problems. Physical illnesses and periods of recovery are recorded in *The House by the Sea*, *Recovering*, and *After The Stroke* and constitute central issues throughout *Endgame* and *Encore*. Also, there is a gradual change in the organization in the journals in regard to frequency of entries. The median number of entries per month increases through the first five journals and then decreases as follows: *Journal of a Solitude*, 6; *The House by the Sea*, 7; *Recovering*, 11; *At Seventy*, 12; *After The Stroke*, 17; *Endgame*, 13; *Encore*, 10.5.

Yet, the journals are also marked by a high degree of consistency in both style and content. Entries are dated and except for in *Journal of a Solitude*, the day of the week is indicated. They typically run to about five hundred words, with the entries in *Journal of a Solitude* tending to be somewhat longer and those in *After The Stroke*, *Endgame* and *Encore* tending to be shorter. Throughout the seven journals, Sarton gives voice to the issues that are articulated in her poetry and fiction: love, friendship, the search for self-knowledge, personal fulfillment, and inner peace and repeatedly draws on what Hunting (1986) has called her salient constellation of images: landscape, music, weather, and art. In all the journals Sarton captures for the reader the sometimes overwhelming influx of correspondence and visitors. The journals also are consistent in tracking the seasons through the eyes of a devoted gardener, with many references to what has come into bloom and what is about to die from lack of water.

This chapter will address a theme that is present throughout the journals but is especially prominent in the journals written when Sarton between the ages of 58 and 70. In Chapter 8, we will return to the Sarton journals and give fuller consideration to the later journals.

The theme that is especially prominent in the earlier journals is the dilemma of reconciling the desire for attachment and the desire for separation. Sarton recognizes this tension as a fundamental feature of human life: "The two greatest yearnings of human beings may be the yearnings for inclusion and the yearnings for distinctness" (1980a, p. 142). The power of the journals lies not in merely acknowledging the importance of the tension between attachment and separateness for people in general, but rather in tracing the emotional upheavals created by these incompatible desires in a particular life.

Intimacy and Solitude in Sarton's Journals

For Sarton the tension between attachment and separation arises in two contexts. The first is in connection with her repeated attempts to establish a lasting, intimate love relationship and the second is in her need for solitude in order to work.

Intimacy

In *Recovering*, Sarton wrote about the feelings generated by her attempts to establish intimate relationships, using a powerful metaphor of movement through geographical space:

> The value of loving someone passionately, often a person very unlike oneself, is that one is taken literally out of one's self on a journey into unknown territory. As in a journey to a foreign country there is culture shock; one often feels lonely, even attacked by the differences. One is also all the time in a state of strange excitement, there are glorious moments, unforgettable scenes that make one tremble with joy and surprise, and there are days of great fatigue when all one longs for is home, to be with the familiar that does not ask for stretching to understand it, which can be taken for granted. Where one can rest. And above all where one is accepted as one is, not stammering in an unfamiliar language, not trying desperately to communicate from one ethos to another. (1980a, p. 204)

During the period covered in the seven journals, Sarton records three such journeys through passionate love relationships. These relationships were with other women of her age. Sarton was aware of the stereotypical responses to the older woman's desire for intimacy with another woman. She wrote:

> Americans are terrified of the very idea of passionate love going on past middle age. Are they afraid of being alive? Do they want to be dead, i.e. *safe*? For of course no one is ever safe when in love. (1973, p. 80, emphasis in original)

And she acknowledged the prevalent notions that to be in love at 60 is ludicrous and that passionate love can be banished in later life. She considers these ideas to be myths that have been around a long time but were never true (1980, p. 204).

Similarly, she was aware that in acknowledging her homosexuality she ran the risk of having everything she wrote analyzed through the lens of sexual preference, of having her novels reduced to one theme:

> What the fear of communism did to destroy lives and to confuse the minds of the innocent to an unbelievable extent under Senator McCarthy's evil influence, the fear of homosexuality appears to be doing now. . . . I have hoped to provide the bridge between women of all ages and kinds. . . . The vision of life in my work is not limited to one segment of humanity or another and it has little to do with sexual proclivity. It does have to do with love, and love has many forms and it is not easy or facile in any of them. (1980a, pp. 80–81)

Nonetheless, she took this risk and wrote openly about her intense passion, her need for intimacy, her desire for "the tangible 'we' when two people live together in amity" (1988, p. 98) and her desolation when such a relationship cannot be achieved.

Sarton's struggles with her passions give insight into the dynamics of intimacy irrespective of the ages or genders of the partners in the relationship. The object of passionate love "focuses the world" (1980a, p. 204) and provides a "gentle river of communion that runs along under all the days" (1980a, p. 239). Such a person can stave off "the quicksand that isolation sometimes creates, a sense of drowning, of being literally engulfed" (1973b, p. 107) and can "bring the world to life" (1977, p. 214). Additionally, some of Sarton's most intense poetry has been inspired by intimate love relationships.

But, for Sarton, intimacy is achieved at a cost: inauthenticity, not being true to her self; in effect, the loss of identity. To Sarton, for whom the creation of a true self is the central purpose of life, such inauthenticity is intolerable:

> The thing is that art doesn't brook a censor and in the relation to those we love if it is not a perfect harmony we have to censor ourselves, keep the demons at bay. Then censorship in one area ends by taking over all areas. (1980a, p. 113)

Also, she recognized that because of her work, she was likely to be misperceived by potential lovers who project their image of May Sarton on to the real person:

> [T]wice in my life people who discovered me through the work, who came to me as admirers and became intimate friends ended by being unable to accept the whole person, the flawed human being because they had somehow fallen in love with an image beside which the reality of a living, suffering being who is not perfect, who is temperamental, who "has no surface" as someone has said of me, became disillusioning. (1980a, p. 123)

Sarton's journals track the mood swings and varying self-evaluations set in motion by the opposing pulls of her desire for intimacy and her desire to be true to herself. They are particularly valuable in providing descriptions of the feelings that arise when the pendulum swings toward the self, that is, the feelings that accompany a decision to break off a love relationship, an event that occurs three times during the 15 years in these journals:

> For a week or more I have been in a state of extreme excitement, as though on the brink of revelation. It began at once as soon as I had decided to bring myself to the point of decision and to break off, not to cling out of need and desperation to something that perhaps was never there. The central person focuses the world and when there is no one to be that, one is at first terrified. But once the decision is made that had to be made, one is free at last to go home to the self, that self which has been censored, without even being aware of it, by the effort to please and to become acceptable to the one one loves. (1980a, pp. 204–205)

The decisions to break off relationships were also accompanied by adjustments in self-concept. At age 60, after the break-up of the relationship that forms an undercurrent to *Journal of A Solitude*, she wrote that she "longed for one person with whom everything could be shared," but was "slowly making my peace with the knowledge that this will never happen" (1973b, p. 157) and that the time had come for her to "have many loves and no love" (1977, p. 262). Yet, she did find another such person. Then, four years later, in *Recovering*, she was dealing with the painful aftermath of that relationship. In a moving passage, she wrote that the "door has closed forever on passionate communion with another human being" and that her body at 67, after a mastectomy, was "the physical evidence of that fact" (1980a, p. 138). But, again, four years later, at age 70, Sarton was in love and once again contending with the competing pulls of the desire for intimacy and the desire to be true to herself.

Thus, during the 20 years covered in the journals, there are successive self-descriptions about being the kind of person who would never be intimate with another, successive predictions that the door to passion had closed forever. Yet, each time the door was opened again.

From the perspective of a reader who knows how the story turns out, it is tempting to view Sarton's statements about her fated isolation as self-deception or as unjustified appeals for sympathy. After all, each time her predictions were proven wrong. But while she was keeping her journals Sarton, of course, could not know how the story would turn out. When she wrote that she would never love again, she was trying to make sense of her life at that moment, to create a narrative that was true to her recent experience. Any such narrative can only be a temporary construction. The journals exemplify the way in which people make meaning out of experience and weave such meanings together to create the story of their lives, a story that is subject to constant revision. We will return to the idea of narratives of the self in Chapter 8.

Solitude

In adulthood, one manifestation of the tension between attachment and separation is the conflict over what is owed

to others versus what is owed to oneself. This conflict typically arises in balancing the competing demands of family and
of work. Family demands involve attentiveness to others'
needs and the fostering of others' growth. Work may also involve meeting others' needs, but, particularly in the case of
writers, it serves principally as a channel for the realization
of self. The tension between obligations to others and obligations to oneself in the arenas of family and work is particularly prominent in Sarton's journals.

Sarton's family obligations do not consist of taking care of
husbands, children, or aging parents. Rather, her family obligations are her obligations; first, toward her successive lovers,
and second, toward her many friends and admirers. She feels
these latter obligations very strongly and knows that she is
enriched by the visits and many appreciative letters she receives. But meeting the needs of lovers and responding to
friends and admirers keep her from her work, her writing,
which requires solitude. Solitude is not only essential for her
work, which provides her livelihood, it is also essential for the
creation of the self which is realized through her work. Thus,
incessant demands to respond to others have the effect of
keeping her from her self.

> It's not that I work all day; it is that the work needs space
> around it. (1977, p. 157)

> For more than a year now I appear to have been fighting for
> myself, fighting to recover the creative being in me, fighting in
> essence to stay alive, not to become silted down in "obligations"
> that are escapes from the far harder obligations to write poems
> and books. (1980a, p. 134)

> "I feel like an animal in a cage, and the cage is kindness. The
> bars are what keep me in prison, what I feel I owe, what some-
> one else needs, the so much wanted *response*" . . . I am nearly
> at the end of what I can ask of this self I bury alive every day
> for the sake of strangers. (1988, p. 242, emphasis in original)

Citing Scott-Maxwell's journal (see Chapter 7), Sarton wrote that the activity of creating the self is a sacred duty (1980a, p. 134) and quoted her father's journal:

> The main purpose of a man's life is to give others what is in him. Such a matter is not a question of selfishness or unselfishness. . . . We only have what we are and we only have what we give. (1980a, p. 35)

Therefore, Sarton is compelled to seek solitude so that she can do her work and realize her true self.

Much of the impact of the journals derives from the descriptions of what solitude is like, its extraordinary possibilities and its terrible costs:

> I am here alone for the first time in weeks to take up my "real life" again at last. . . . When I am alone the flowers are really seen; I can pay attention to them. They are felt presences. Without them I would die. (1973b, p. 11)

> We are one, the house and I, and I am happy to be alone—time to think, time to be. (1973b, p. 81)

> There are compensations for not being in love—solitude grows richer for me every year. (1977, p. 61)

The creative possibilities afforded by solitude do not mean that it leads to continuous inner harmony. Quite to the contrary, Sarton's solitude (particularly during the period of *Journal of A Solitude*) meant that she was open to "attacks from within" (1973b, p. 16).

> My need to be alone is balanced against my fear of what will happen when suddenly I enter the huge empty silence if I cannot find support there. I go up to Heaven and down to Hell in an hour. . . . (1973b, p. 12)

Also, many expressions in the journals reveal desperate loneliness, "loneliness like starvation" (1977, p. 203), loneliness because she cannot live with the person she loves (1980a, p. 239)

Her solitude is experienced as painful when she thinks about having sole responsibility for all housekeeping and maintenance chores, tasks which can become particularly difficult during New Hampshire and Maine winters.

Solitude is also experienced as painful when there is no one with whom to share joy. For example, in 1972 Sarton was alone when she received in the mail copies of her book of poetry *A Grain of Mustard Seed*. About that experience she wrote: "I felt let down to be alone with this newborn babe, to have no one to whom I could show it" (1973b, p. 87).

Her solitude is also experienced as painful during periods of illness, such as the six month period of recovery from her stroke. The loneliness experienced during this protracted period of illness was, as much as anything, due to being deprived of her self, and of being unable to write, rather than to merely being alone.

The "attacks from within," the loneliness and self-criticism are not merely fleeting thoughts which are then put aside. The entries for months at a time are dominated by unhappiness. However, even in the midst of periods of unhappiness she maintains an optimism about the ultimate usefulness of her ordeal:

> [S]ometimes one has simply to endure a period of depression
> for what it may hold of illumination if one can live through it,
> attentive to what it exposes or demands. (1973b, p. 16)

Also, she forces herself to be open to negative feelings because of her faith that "the courage to despair" (1973b, p. 22) is essential to creativity.

Sarton's valuing of solitude, despite the pain associated with it, makes her work especially meaningful to readers who are also leading lives of solitude or who wish for such lives. In the journals, Sarton records her gratitude that readers take comfort from her accounts of the solitary life, but she is also aware how easily such a life can be romanticized. She is critical of young people to whom she may represent "a role model that is dangerous rather than helpful" (1980a, p. 32). She does not want to be misconstrued as advocating solitude for its own sake. Rather, "if one does choose solitude it must be for a purpose other than mere self-seeking" (1980a, p. 32). From the perspective of her life at age 70, she recognized that "we all have our nostalgias for the giving up of 'the world'" (1984, p. 26). She warned her readers and correspondents repeatedly during the fifteen years covered in the journals that the solitary life should not be envied, and it especially should not be pursued by the young:

> I did not begin to live alone till I was forty-five, and had "lived" in the sense of passionate friendships and love affairs very richly for twenty-five years. I had a huge amount of life to think about and to digest, and above all, I was a *person* by then and knew what I wanted of my life. (1977, p. 135, emphasis in original)

The idea of a fruitful tension between total independence and involvement with others and with the world has also been discussed by Sarton in her essay on poets and poetry, "The School of Babylon." The essay is organized around the idea of the tensions Sarton experiences in the process of writing a poem and the parallel tensions of daily life. Among the latter, she cites the tension between the public and the private person. She views this as a "not unfruitful" tension and observes admiringly that Yeats's "assaults on the world" as founder of the Abbey Theatre and as a senator "helped him to forge his style" (1980b, pp. 5–6).

Much as she needs her separateness, she recognizes in the journals that total independence is not desirable:

At what price would total independence be bought? That's the rub! I am conscious of the fruitful tension set up between me and anyone for whom I care. . . . I learn by being *in relation to.* (1973b, p. 107, emphasis in original)

And in a letter to a young admirer, she wrote:

Agreed that human relationships are often painful, always maybe collisions, but through them we grow. How do we grow otherwise? You yourself say in this letter, "It is in my times alone that I straighten things out" . . . exactly. But there would be nothing to straighten out if you had no relationships. (1980a, p. 33)

The complex relationship between the desires for intimacy and solitude is especially well reflected in a passage from *After the Stroke*. After recovering from more than six months of illness stemming from a stroke, heart fibrillation, undiagnosed diverticulitis, and the side effects of medication, Sarton wrote:

Because I am well I no longer suffer from the acute loneliness I felt all spring and summer until now. Loneliness because in spite of all the kindnesses and concerns of so many friends there was no one who could fill the hole at the center of my being—only myself could fill it by becoming whole again. It was loneliness in essence for the *self.* (1988, p. 124, emphasis in original)

In this passage, written at age 74, Sarton is saying that her lifelong project of creating her self has resulted in a feeling for her self that is akin to feelings she has had toward those with whom she has been intimate. Just as, in the past, she experienced loneliness rooted in the absence of others, here she describes the experience of a loneliness rooted in the absence of her self. An intimate other can focus the world and stave off the quicksand that isolation sometimes creates, but such a person cannot fill the hole at the center of her being.

Her need for others is great, but, in a certain sense, her need for her self is greater.

COMMENTARY

Attachment and Separateness in Psychoanalytic Theory

Personality theorists who have developed typologies of motivational constructs fall into three camps: (1) those suggesting a plurality of basic human tendencies, such as Abraham Maslow, who proposed a hierarchy of six basic needs, (2) those arguing for the primacy of a single motive, such as Carl Rogers, who put the striving for self-actualization at the center of his view of human nature, and (3) those advocating motivational dichotomies (McAdams, 1988). Psychologists in the latter group typically propose that the primary forces in personality exist in a dialectical tension. Dialectical theories commonly imply that human beings are, by their motivational nature, beset with conflict and that the goal of development and therapy is a reconciliation of opposites. Moreover, although a variety of pairs of opposing characteristics could be posited as fundamental, several prominent theorists have arrived at the same basic opposition, the tension between attachment and separation, as the most parsimonious way to characterize human nature.

An essential cornerstone of Freud's theory of personality is the concept of innate instinctual drives. The theme of drives, of how they are transformed and blocked, permeates Freud's writings. After much revision of his theories, in his later writings Freud advanced the idea of two fundamental, unconscious, innate, instinctual motives which he labeled Eros and Thanatos. The aim of Eros is to attach: to establish unities and preserve them, to bind together. The aim of Thanatos is to separate: to undo connections and to destroy (Freud, 1949).

Eros was understood to be the force behind a person's love of self and love of others. It lies behind the instincts of self-preservation and preservation of the species. Thanatos was understood to be the force behind what Freud came to understand as people's natural aggressiveness toward both self and others. The two motives, although they are in opposition, are nonetheless intertwined. Destruction and creation are inseparable. They may combine toward achievement of the same end, but they no less often create conflicting impulses. The flow of cooperation and opposition between these two forces produces the phenomenon of life—to which death puts an end. Eating, for example, is a process of destruction with the purpose of incorporation. Similarly, sexual impulses are erotic, but also include aggressive and destructive demands. Freud's version of the tension between Eros and Thanatos puts conflict between attachment and separation at the center of human nature and shows the multiple ways that the desire for attachment and the desire for separation are satisfied and thwarted by any particular course of action. Freud was masterful in describing what Peter Gay has called the "ubiquitous working of ambivalence in mental life" (Gay, 1988, p. 259).

Otto Rank proposed a motivational dichotomy similar to Freud's, but built around the ideas of acquired fears, rather than innate instincts. Rank's ideas have received a compelling exposition by Ernest Becker (1973). Becker reviewed the psychoanalytic insights about childhood, drawn upon by Rank, which support the notion that life is shaped by the opposing pulls of two fears, the fear of death and the fear of life. The fear of death is characterized as the affective aspect of the tendency toward self-preservation. In other words, Rank, following Freud (and Darwin), asserts that organisms strive to preserve themselves against the forces of disintegration. But in human beings there is an emotional side to this striving, the fear of death. From early childhood, human beings, unlike animals, are aware of the possibility of ceasing to exist. Psychoanalysis pointed out the extent to which the child's inner world was filled with this fear. The child's fear stems partly from its utter helplessness, but it also arises from confusion about cause-and-effect relationships and extreme unreality about the limits of its powers.

> The child lives in a situation of utter dependence; and when his needs are met it must seem to him that he has magical powers, real omnipotence. If he experiences pain, hunger, or discomfort, all he has to do is to scream and he is relieved and lulled by gentle, loving sounds. He is a magician and a telepath who has only to mumble and to imagine and the world turns to his desires. (Becker, 1973, p. 18)

But the penalty for such perceptions is that in a magical world where a thought or wish causes things to happen anything can happen to anyone—including the child. The argument is that children, therefore, live with the fear that annihilation is only a thought or wish away. As time goes on this fear is repressed, but as with other repressed affects, it does not disappear from the unconscious. Rather, defense processes are established to ward off this fear, the most notable defense process being one of reversal, in which the fear energizes the individual's striving to expand into the world and take pleasure in unfolding capacities.

> The organism works actively against its own fragility by seeking to expand and perpetuate itself in living experience; instead of shrinking, it moves toward more life. (Becker, 1973, p. 21)

The ultimate extension of such striving is heroism, which in Rank's and Becker's view is essentially having the courage to face the world on one's own terms, the courage to be an individual, to be separate. The desire for separation, therefore, can be characterized as a reflex of the fear of death.

The desire to move out into the world, to be different, to stand out, is held in check by a second fear, the fear of life.

The problem that gives rise to the fear of life is that, in relation to the vastness of creation, human beings are tiny, vulnerable creatures. Life is cheap. Any given person is caught up in the myriad of cross purposes of the planet. Life can suck one up, sap energies, take away self-control, give new experience too quickly, load one up with too many responsibilities which need great strength to bear.

The feeling of being frightened by the vastness of creation is evoked in the following lines from Pascal:

> When I consider the brief span of my life, merged in eternity before and after, the little room I fill and can even see, engulfed in the infinite immensity of spaces which I know not and which know not me, I fall into fear. (Pascal, 1950, p. 173)

Another poetic expression of the fear of life is found in the famous lines from the eighth Psalm:

> When I behold Thy heavens, the work of thy fingers, the moon and the stars, which thou hast established; what is man, that Thou art mindful of him? And the son of man, that Thou thinkest of him?

To ward off and defend against the fear of life, from childhood on people seek protection by becoming part of, by merging with, something larger and more powerful than themselves. The fear of being overwhelmed by the world and by experience leads people to seek comfort, security, and serenity and to desire to merge with an other—it leads them, in short, to attachment.

Thus, this view of the human condition holds that human life is in a state of tension between two great fears, the fear of death and the fear of life. The fear of death pushes toward the expansion of life and separation from others, but the fear of life pushes toward stability and relatedness. We are driven toward situations that provide automatic equanimity, but we are simultaneously driven toward situations that disrupt equanimity. But such anxiety provoking situations make us anxious and drive us back toward the familiar and the secure.

The fear of life impels people to subsume themselves into collectivities and in this respect operates like Freud's Eros. The fear of death drives people outward, toward mastery of the environment, and in this respect operates like Freud's Thanatos.

Gender Differences in Attachment and Separation

The motivational dichotomy presented by Freud and Rank is also elaborated by the psychologist Bakan (1966). Though largely ignored at the time of its publication, this work has received increasing recognition by those interested in personality development over the life course (Kegan, 1982; Kotre, 1984; McAdams, 1988). Bakan uses the terms *agency* and *communion* to express his basic dialectical opposition. He considers these to be the two fundamental modalities of living forms. Agency represents the existence of an organism as an individual and communion the participation of the individual in some larger organism of which the individual is a part. They are the functions associated with the separations of cells, organs, or individuals from one another and the unions which may be formed among them. The agency modality is involved in the processes of differentiation, specialization, and separation of function within and between organismic units, whereas communion is involved in a variety of relationships among organismic units.

> Agency manifests itself in self-protection, self-assertion, and self-expansion; communion manifests itself in the sense of being at one with other organisms. Agency manifests itself in the formation of separations; communion in the lack of separations. Agency manifests itself in isolation, alienation, and

aloneness; communion in contact, openness, and union. Agency
manifests itself in the urge to master; communion in noncon-
tractual cooperation. Agency manifests itself in the repression
of thought, feeling, and impulse; communion in the lack and
removal of repression. (Bakan, 1966, p. 15)

The modalities of agency and communion are presumed to
exist at a level of generality that transcends the biological,
psychological, and social but which is manifested in each of
them. In wide-ranging essays, Bakan applies the agency–
communion dichotomy to the biology of cancer, the figure of
Satan in Western religious thought, the emergence of the
Protestant Ethic, and psychological differences between men
and women.

The idea of a tendency toward psychological agency (and,
therefore, separation) in men and psychological communion
(and attachment) in women has been developed more fully in
recent works that provide feminist critiques of research on
human development.

Gilligan (1982) has argued that major psychological theorists, including Freud, Erikson, Vaillant, Levinson and Kohlberg, though ostensibly employing a value-neutral scientific
stance, have labeled as human what is actually masculine
development and have ignored the distinctive theme of concern for relationships that pervades women's lives. She provides evidence that moral reasoning in men and women develops along alternative pathways and that women's moral
development is based upon a logic of equity in relationships
and an ethic of care, whereas that of men is based on a logic
of equality and an ethic of rights.

Gilligan associates these different voices of moral reasoning with the themes of attachment and separation in the development of gender identity. She views separation as the
hallmark of the development of masculinity, while femininity
is defined through attachment. Male gender identity is threatened by intimacy, but female gender identity is threatened

by separation. For Gilligan, attachment and separation anchor the cycle of human life and constitute a reiterative counterpoint in human experience. She argues that "male and female voices typically speak of the importance of different truths, the former of the role of separation as it defines and empowers the self, the latter of the ongoing process of attachment that creates and sustains human community" (Gilligan, 1982, p. 156).

Franz and White (1985) elaborate on Gilligan's critique of Erikson's model of psychosocial development. They concur that Erikson's theory is male-centered and does not adequately account for the development of various forms of interpersonal connectedness. Through an analysis of each of Erikson's eight stages, they show how Erikson's theory works best in dealing with issues of separation and individuation that are central to male ego development but only weakly addresses the developmental trajectory of the process of attachment. These authors propose to replace Erikson's single path approach with a double helix model of psychosocial development in which the two distinct, but interconnected, strands of separation and attachment ascend in a spiral representing the life cycle. Each stage in this model represents an intrapsychic developmental change in both separation and attachment, with experiences in one realm having implications for the other. By specifying the developmental dilemmas associated with attachment through the entire course of life, Franz and White illuminate the developmental paths taken by both men and women.

An investigation of women's ways of knowing by Belenky, Clinchy, Goldberger and Tarule (1986) led to the formulation of five epistemological perspectives from which women know and view the world. Their discussion of one of these perspectives, which they term procedural knowing, extends Gilligan's assertions about the place of attachment and separation in the lives of women and men. Belenky et al. distinguish between *separate knowing*, which involves impersonal processes for assessing truth, and *connected knowing*, which is based on establishing a relationship with the object of knowledge. The essence of separate knowing is analysis, objectivity and the distancing of the person from the object of knowledge in order to preclude bias. Connected knowing, in contrast, involves a capacity for empathy, the imaginative extension of one's understanding, and what Nodding (1984) has termed *receptive rationality*. Although some of the women in the Belenky et al. study were capable of skillfully practicing the impersonal procedures required by separate knowing, few were comfortable with this epistemological position. Many women, however, took naturally to connected knowing as a means of obtaining knowledge that felt real, that is, that was personal, particular and grounded in first hand experience.

David Gutmann has explored the attachment-separation dichotomy in investigations of the differing developmental paths followed by men and women as they approach later life (Gutmann, 1987). On the basis of cross-cultural psychological data and clinical work with both men and women, he concurs with the basic notion of a predisposition toward psychological agency in men and communion in women, but only through mid-life. Gutmann provides extensive evidence that in later life, there is a tendency for men to become what Bakan would term more communal and for women to become more agentic. His argument, therefore, is that the idea that separation is the dominant theme in men's lives and attachment the dominant theme in women's is based on a constricted view of the life course. In the second half of life, he posits a contrasexual shift, a movement toward what he terms the normal androgyny of later life. Support for this finding has also been presented by Daniel Levinson in his study of mid-life men (Levinson et al., 1978).

The accumulation of evidence pointing toward an association between agency as a male predisposition and communion as a female predisposition (through a substantial portion of the life course) leads to the question of what might cause such a difference to arise. Important contributions to our understanding of this phenomenon have been made by Dinnerstein (1977) and by Chodorow (1978; 1989). Drawing on psychoanalytic concepts, both of these theorists attribute the differential emphasis on attachment and separation in the lives of women and men to early experience and, specifically, to the early experience of being nurtured by female caregivers. Their argument is that from the first moments of life little girls receive most of their care from a person of the same gender. Female identity formation, therefore, takes place in the context of a relationship of similarity. In coming to understand themselves as female, young girls experience themselves as like their mothers. For girls, identity formation coincides with attachment. Boys, however, in coming to see themselves as male must separate from their female parent. For them, separation is central to the emergence of a sense of self. Both Dinnerstein and Chodorow argue that this fundamental difference in early experience reverberates throughout life and is the origin of the male tendency toward agency and the female tendency toward communion.

Attachment Theory

The tension between the basic opposition and interrelatedness of attachment and separation is also seen in the rich line of research known as attachment theory (Ainsworth, 1989; Bowlby, 1988; Mahler, Pine, & Bergman, 1975). This research deals primarily with development in early childhood, but it has been applied to developmental issues across the life span. Its intellectual roots are in both ethology and psychoanalysis. Research carried out within the framework of attachment theory has documented the profound developmental importance of the formation of healthy attachments during the first months of life. Healthy attachment is viewed not as dependence, but rather as a secure base for exploration of the physical and social environment. From an attachment theory perspective, healthy early attachments create the ground from which separation can occur. The stresses that invariably arise in the course of exploration of the environment can be alleviated through the availability of attachment figures, which may be actual others or internal representations.

In a fascinating critique of this large body of research Storr 1988) questions the emphasis attachment theory places on interpersonal relationships as the chief source of human happiness, particularly in adulthood. He argues that attachment theory gives insufficient attention to the need for separation in the lives of adults, especially in the lives of creative individuals. Storr's critique of attachment theory is directed at restoring the developmental significance of the other pole of the attachment-separation dichotomy and balancing attachment theory's emphasis on the central importance of interpersonal relationships with an equal emphasis on the value of solitude and the capacity to be alone in the lives of adults.

Sarton's Journals and the Tensions of Attachment

The main idea of this chapter is that in her journals, Sarton reveals herself to be susceptible to that which, according to an important line of theorizing about the human condition, ails us all: the conflict between the longing for attachment and the longing for separation. Depending on the theory one chooses, these longings are viewed as deriving from innate instincts, acquired fears, or the fundamental modalities of living forms. The longings for both attachment and separation constitute one of the dichotomies at the heart of human existence. As Mahoney (1991) has argued, the self-constructing living systems that we call human beings consist, both biologically and psychologically, of subsystems that operate on the basis of opponent processes in states of dynamic tension. Each individual is always doing his or her best to keep opponent processes in dynamic balance. In adulthood, the conflict between the opponent processes of attachment and separation is translated into the dilemmas people face about intimacy and identity. Movement toward intimacy may satisfy the need for attachment but may frustrate the longing for separateness. Movement toward the formation of a distinct identity, toward becoming one's own man or woman, may satisfy the longing for separateness, but frustrate the longing for attachment. Moreover, because of the complex ways in which actions relate to motives, any given action may relate to both attachment and separateness. For example, in adulthood, people learn about themselves—in effect, create their selves—through their self-initiated involvements with others, involvements that place demands on them for time and energy. But those involvements, if left unchecked, can draw a person totally away from the self. A measure of separateness must be preserved in order to develop the self and, thereby, be able to give to others the best one has to offer. The question we all face is where to draw the line.

The principal value of Sarton's journals is not in providing answers, but, rather, in holding this conflict up to the light. Sarton does not tell us anything about the conflict between attachment and separateness that we could not, potentially, have drawn out of our own experience. But she does articulate the dilemma in ways that are beyond most people's capabilities, and, in so doing, she helps us to comprehend the pushes and pulls of the motives of attachment and separateness in our own lives. Moreover, she keeps the contradictory tensions of attachment and separateness alive within her into her seventh and eighth decades. Through an act of will, what Sarton at one point refers to as "divine discontent," (Sarton, 1973b, p. 22) she refuses to accept the solutions that are readily at hand—repression of her opposing wishes or the conscious abandonment of her longing for either intimacy or solitude.

Not everyone will or can give voice to deeply held fears and desires. Sarton is compelled to do so out of her faith that "pri-

vate dilemmas are, if deeply examined, universal" and her belief that she possesses "the vehicle for expressing them, the
talent" (Sarton, 1973b, p. 59). Her steadfast adherence to this
faith through all seven of her journals makes clear that the dilemma of attachment and separateness does not necessarily
vanish in the later years.

Doris Grumbach: Recovery from Despair

5

Doris Grumbach has been a teacher, literary critic, biographer, and novelist. With the publication of her book *Coming Into the End Zone* (1991), she has added the journal form to her published writing and has produced an excellent example of a personal journal of later life.*

PROFILE

Grumbach was born in 1918 in New York City and married at age 23. She served in the WAVES in San Francisco during World War II and subsequently had four children. She moved with her husband and family to Albany, New York, and began teaching, first, at a private school, then at the College of Saint Rose, where she was on the faculty from 1955 to 1973. During her years of teaching and raising her family, she com-

---

*Subsequent to the preparation of this chapter, Doris Grumbach published a second personal journal, *Extra Innings* (1993), covering the events of her life from September 1991 to September 1992, the year in which she celebrated her 74th birthday.

pleted two novels, but she became recognized principally as a book reviewer and critic. In 1973 she divorced and moved to Washington, D.C., to work as literary editor of *The New Republic*, a position that she continued until 1975. She then assumed a faculty post as Professor of American Literature at American University, where she remained until the events recorded in the journal.

Her criticism has appeared in many publications including the *New York Times Book Review*, *The Saturday Review*, *The Chronicle of Higher Education*, and *The New Republic*. During the 1980s, her voice and critical insights became widely known through her work as regular book reviewer for "Morning Edition" on National Public Radio. During her years in Washington, she also was co-owner, with her companion Sybil Slater, of Wayside Books, a store that specialized in fine used books.

In 1967, Grumbach became the center of a controversy over her biography of Mary McCarthy. The book became the subject of a threatened lawsuit before its publication and a sharply divided critical debate after its release. The book argues that the characters and events in McCarthy's novels parallel persons and events in McCarthy's life to a far greater degree than had been previously recognized. Difficulties arose when McCarthy protested against some of the information Grumbach had included in the manuscript. Intimate biographical details had been obtained by Grumbach from interviews and a detailed memorandum written by McCarthy. McCarthy claimed the information had been provided for Grumbach's "enlightenment," not for use in the biography. McCarthy was successful in suppressing material from the book.

Subsequent to the controversy over the McCarthy biography, Grumbach returned to fiction and completed the novels *Chamber Music* (1979), *Missing Person* (1981), *The Ladies* (1985), and *The Magician's Girl* (1987). These novels were generally well received. Each in its own way elaborated an approach to fiction in which the facts of the lives of notable contemporary and historical figures are used as the basis for the lives of fictional characters. The fictional characters may be modeled on specific individuals, as in *Chamber Music* and *The Ladies*, or may be created by blending characteristics of several different persons, as in *The Magician's Girl*. The characters tend to be intelligent people who are unable to use their knowledge to enjoy fulfilling relationships or satisfying lives (Matuz, 1991).

THE JOURNAL

Grumbach's diary is organized into twelve sections, one for each month between July 1988, when she turned 70, and July 1989 (there is one section for June and July 1989). With two exceptions, the separate entries within each month are not dated. The two exceptions are October 10, 1988, a day on which she fell and broke her shoulder, and July 12, 1989, the day of her 71st birthday.

There is an overall narrative structure to the diary. When the diary begins Grumbach is in a period of emotional distress. It was a time of her life in which she saw "no redeeming moments." The purpose of the journal, she stated, was the hope that in the recording process she would find a positive value to living so long (p. 12). One fourth of the book is devoted to the July entries and exploration of the bases for the feelings of despair. Subsequently, there is a gradual shift in the tone of the entries. The mood lightens and the entries for each month tend to become shorter. By her 71st birthday, Grumbach has recovered her sense of purpose and found the positive value to living that was missing a year earlier. Of course, neither the reader nor the writer could have predicted how the story would unfold. It is only in retrospect that the narrative structure is evident.

Two key events during the year, aside from the birthdays that frame the diary and the shoulder accident, are an October trip to Paris and a January trip to Mayan sites in Mexico. But the most significant events in terms of a change in life structure are Grumbach's decision to move from Washington, D.C., to Maine and the move itself, which occurred in May 1989.

Interestingly, Grumbach labels the book a memoir, not a journal or diary. The book could be considered a memoir in that many entries are devoted to recounting incidents from the past and describing people from earlier periods in her life. But the book is firmly rooted in the succession of day-to-day events, with each entry clearly identified as having been written in a particular month. Moreover, these day-to-day events form the basis of the author's reflections on herself and her place in the world. Accordingly, the book fits squarely within the definition of personal journal.

Grumbach's skill as a writer is evident throughout the book. There are especially effective descriptions of her visits to the Mayan temples and of her new surroundings in Maine. What makes the book particularly valuable for studying the experience of aging is the way Grumbach turns her powers of description to examination of the physical aspects of aging and to the bases for her feelings of despair.

Grumbach's is a world of writers, writing, and reading. Numerous entries mention writers she knows and reflect on the work of writing and the temperaments and aspirations of writers. There are frequent references to books she has reviewed on National Public Radio and to the burden (and sheer physical weight) of all the books she receives in the mail. Despite the complaints, her love of books and her passion for well-made books is quite evident.

A notable characteristic of Grumbach's style is her mordant self-mockery. Humorous entries in which she makes fun of herself are found throughout the book, but are typified by the following from June/July 1989.

National Public Radio is still airing tapes of reviews I did last month. In the market I meet a chap who is behind me in line. He hears me speak to a clerk, and recognizes my voice.

'Are you Doris Grumbach?' he asks.

'I am.'

'Well, I want to tell you. I listen to you in the morning on the radio while I pee.'

I thank him, thinking that this must be as much fame as I will ever achieve. What greater recognition can come to me? (p. 232)

Age Changes in Body and Mind

At 70, Grumbach has already experienced significant changes in physical and cognitive functioning. She candidly describes the changes in her body when, on the day of her 70th birthday, she happens to catch sight of herself in a full-length mirror.

Now I look, hard. I see the pull of gravity on the soft tissues of my breasts and buttocks. I see the heavy rings that encircle my neck like Ubangi jewelry. I notice bones that seem to have thinned and shrunk. Muscles appear to be watered down. The walls of my abdomen, like Jericho, have softened and now press outward. There is nothing lovely about the sight of me. (pp. 52–53)

Other bodily changes she observes include arms that will no longer lift her "thickened" body out of chairs or out of the bath, a back that hurts under the stress of lifting or bending or "sometimes for no reason at all," teeth loosely rooted in gums and irritations of pollen and dust in eyes, nose, and throat (p. 81) and "cholesterol-laden arteries" (p. 101).

She is sharply aware of slowing of her gait. She describes herself as "shaky on her pins" and resents the old speed she has lost, because her slower pace gives her age away. She says that her resentment of her loss of speed has soured her outlook on speed so that she loathes "fast cars, planes, rapid talkers, swift up and down escalators, athletes, the computer's cursor, the publisher of instant books, the producer of 'new and improved' products seemingly days after the original was marketed" (p. 20).

Grumbach's shakiness on her pins relates to her proclivity for falls. She always fears slipping, stumbling, and being hurt. Apparently, the tendency for falls started earlier in life, but it is a special concern at her present age. In an August entry she acknowledged having broken ankles twice and having sprained or strained them many times. Then in October while on a trip to New York, the fears she expressed in August are validated. In the late afternoon of October 10, after sitting and having coffee on the benches at 44th Street and the Avenue of the Americas, she stands up and "inexplicably" falls on her face.

This incident is told within the framework of a powerful narrative. From her bench, Grumbach had been observing a street lady who had been eating a hot dog and talking to herself. The woman's appearance and manner are described in detail.

> Her eyebrows are crusted and red, the same flush that covers her light-brown skin and culminates in an angry red ball at the end of her nose. Her body is very thin under a coat composed, like her hair, of parts that are pinned together. . . . She moves as if her steps were painful. Her face suggests misery and resentment. . . . She wipes her mouth and her nose on her fingers and then puts them in her mouth. I shudder. (p.109)

After Grumbach fell, she remained on the sidewalk, feeling intense pain in her ankle and left shoulder. "I lie there, seeing two sets of feet in well-shined shoes pass me by without breaking stride" (p. 110).

It was the repulsive street lady who came to help.

Then I see a brown hand near my face and hear the street lady's rough voice say: "Here. Hold on here." . . . She pulls hard, I hold tight, I am up, dizzy. She puts her arm around my shoulders and puts me down on the bench. She sits beside me. (p. 110)

For the next hour she and the street lady, Nancy, talked about life on the streets and in a welfare hotel and about Grumbach's pain and dizziness. Grumbach was finally able to rise and get to her planned meeting with her daughter. The next day she learned she had broken her shoulder. The memory of Nancy became less distinct. She asked herself if she would look her up the next time she came to New York and answered, "probably not, knowing how such resolves usually end for me" (p. 111).

In addition to the age changes in physical appearance, speed, reaction time and muscle coordination, Grumbach has also experienced changes in sensory functioning and cognition. She acknowledges a substantial decline in hearing ability, which has resulted in her acquiring two hearing aids, "two disturbing, overmagnifying instruments" (p. 20). Hearing loss has its compensations, however. She is less able to hear raucous noises of her Washington neighborhood and at some plays "it is a comfortable kind of literary criticism to turn the little buttons off so I hear less of the inane dialogue being exchanged by unbelievable characters in a dull and unconvincing situation" (p. 21).

Age changes in cognition are recorded in the journal. She reads more slowly and believes her memory has declined. When younger, her memory was excellent, "a perfect photographic memory." Now her memory is much diminished, "like a hard disk that suddenly fails to deliver what has been stored there" (p. 23). She is aware of lapsing into repetitiveness, of forgetting to whom a story had been told: "At the end of the conversation I find myself beginning a narrative I have already told her. Horrified, I withdraw as inobtrusively as I can and say goodbye" (p.125). For a writer, a decline in memory is particularly frustrating because it constitutes an impediment to work.

> The connections I make are hard-won, sudden flashes from the past, lucky effluvia from the ripe, aging compost heap that is my mind. . . . I feel grateful for the arrival of small pieces of information, now that the lifelong storage system of my personal computer is often down. (p. 23)

Closeness to Death and Survivor Guilt

Death has become a continuing presence in Grumbach's life during her seventy-first year. She is reminded that for Poe time was the unstoppable tread of death and comments that she hears this tread more clearly than she once did "when the steps were muffled by activity and love" (p. 55). She feels she is near the end of her life, especially during the low emotional period of July 1988: "How can it be . . . I am so close to the end when, a short time ago, I was just beginning?" (p. 51). Although a shift in time perspective involving increasing concern about "time left to live" is shared by many people from middle age onward (Neugarten, 1968) the comment is particularly germane to Grumbach, who feels she did not begin her life as a novelist until she returned to fiction writing at age 53.

Grumbach plays a sort of betting game with herself relating to the idea that she is close to death. It is a game which is reminiscent of Kübler-Ross's bargaining stage in the process of dying: "I never say yes to invitations to speak or read or teach if the proposed time is a month or two ahead, believing that there might be a chance I will be living when the time comes. But a year from now is very safe" (pp. 53–54). Whereas in Kübler-Ross's theory, people who are dying bargain with God to allow them to live to a significant life event, such as a child or grandchild's marriage or graduation, Grumbach makes a bargain with herself that she can safely accept invitations for future appearances because she will not have to follow through with the necessary preparations, as she will be dead. Of course, if she loses the bet, she does have to do the work, but the consolation is that she is alive.

It is not only her subjective experience of her age that makes Grumbach close to death. In terms of the people in her circle of friends from the world of writing and publishing, 1988 and 1989 were plague years. The first entry in the journal is about the deaths of friends from AIDS, and throughout the journal there are entries naming other friends who have succumbed, the disease having "violently erased" (p. 14) their lives. She discusses the obituaries of AIDS victims, with their oblique, almost coded references to the disease, and she attends memorial services for her young friends who died during the year. These are wrenching experiences and she is deeply pained by the loss of these young lives. With the logic used by people in periods of unhappiness, the loss of these young lives leads her to question the worthwhileness of her own survival. Why should she, at her advanced age, live, and her young friends suffer and unjustly die? The guilt she feels as a survivor is expressed particularly strongly during the first part of the journal, the period in which she questions whether there is a positive value to living. Later in the year, she seems able to mourn the deaths and acknowledge the "terrible realities of this decade" (p. 189) without expressing guilt about her own survival.

Despair and Hope

The central theme of the journal is the despair that dominates the beginning of the journal and the gradual recovery of belief in the value of living that emerges as the year progresses. The losses she has experienced are partly due to the deaths of friends and relatives. But she has also experienced the loss of the internal anchoring of her life, losses of faith, optimism, physical pleasure, and great expectations (p. 27).

What she has had faith in has been "removed, changed, deleted" (p. 70). At another point, she expresses scorn at the efforts of writers to do something meaningful.

> We [writers] struggle to write what we feel compelled to, we believe we have something to say to the world. Twenty-five years later we are dead, our name is forgotten, our work, if it is noticed at all, is acknowledged with condescension and scorn. Why do we care now? I find I do not really know. (p. 114)

Grumbach gives us a glimpse of the identity struggle that accompanies her sense of despair. She writes: "'Who am I?' Or the question that runs parallel to it: 'What has my life meant?'" (p. 70). For someone of her age, she is saying, the question of identity coincides with the question of what one's life has amounted to, what that life has meant. Sadly, at this point in the journal Grumbach's answer is that all she amounts to is her name, "a first name from my parents, the other part from my husband, not much of my own" (p. 70).

Grumbach is aware of the despondent tenor of many of the entries. In a December entry, she characterizes the journal as a "straying trail of blood, with not much optimism that it will dry up and disappear, or turn to Hansel's white bread crumbs that will lead the reader out of the black forest into light and hope" (p. 137)

During the period of depression that dominates the early part of the year, there are several references to her sense of increased responsiveness to her environment.

> In bed, I think about surroundings. Now that I am old, they seem to have suddenly become of greater importance to me. . . . When I was young I was hardly aware of where I was. (p. 43)

Unfortunately, during this period of increasing responsiveness to the environment, her Washington neighborhood is becoming more and more threatening. The journal includes descriptions of an attack on a woman on the street outside Grumbach's home, the theft of her car by a teenage joyrider, and several robberies and break-ins at Wayward Books. Her increasing responsiveness to the environment prevents her from adopting a philosophical stance toward these events. She notes her rising feeling of paranoia. These external events are experienced as attacks from within (p. 95) and reinforce her sense of despair.

In one of the entries on her 70th birthday, Grumbach presents an image that dramatically captures both the unhappiness and sense of purposelessness that predominate for her at that moment and her distress over the physical aspects of aging. She describes an occasion when she was driving in Florida and pulled over to look at an elongated boxcar with grillwork at the sides. "There . . . are six tired, sick-looking lions, with yellow, aged manes and flabby, ineffectual paws. Their eyes are full of tears" (p. 55). The lions are an attraction designed to call attention to some used cars being sold by their keeper, who is outfitted in knickers, jungle shirt and whip. The keeper flashes his whip across the lions' faces. "They stare back at him, understanding perfectly but too weary, too sick, too wise to obey."

> I stand still, enclosed like the abject lions in the unreasonable quarters of my old body, confined to the bars and sawdust of a future that can end only in the black light of oblivion. What remains of their lives is a dirty joke, told with a snicker by an obscene keeper in cowboy boots, holding a taunting whip. What remains of mine is not much more elevated: There are too few years left to make another life. My age is my cage; only death can free me. (p. 56)

If the despair captured in this image and in the passages noted above persisted throughout the year (as it does in the lives of many depressed people) the journal would constitute a valuable contribution to our understanding of the inner experience of loss of a sense of purpose in late life. However, *Coming into the End Zone* provides more than a picture of despair, because during the year the author regains a sense of the value of living. As we read the book we do not know how things will turn out. But, as it does turn out, the diary constitutes a narrative of both despair and the recovery of hope.

The change is gradual. By October, the entries tend more toward reminiscing and less toward expressions of resentment about her age or physical condition, although there are still many dour moments. In November, there are entries describing her enjoyment of the trip to Paris. These stand in sharp contrast to a July entry in which she writes about being too old to enjoy leaving home. And then, in December, there is the dramatic, dizzying decision to buy a house in Maine.

The purchase of the house came about while Grumbach and Sybil Slater were on a Christmas visit to friends in Maine. The idea of a move to Maine had been broached in a letter they received in the fall. While on the visit, they agreed to look at various properties. "Neither of us thought about immediate purchase and relocation" (p. 144). But they both fell in love with a house on a hill above a cove. "We were indeed lost. Without ever having set foot in the house, we knew instantly we wanted to live on this cove, in sight of all that varied, layered beauty and blue winter water" (p. 145). The next day they signed the contract.

The purchase of the new house is accompanied by the recovery of optimism and a different perspective on her aging body: "Even with all the dire anatomical warnings that arrive on occasion, optimism rules one's decisions" (p. 146). She interprets the move in light of a similar successful uprooting from earlier period of her life.

> Once before, when I was fifty-four, I left the life I had led for more than thirty years, my marriage, my longtime tenured teaching job, everyone I knew, the city I had lived in or near

for more than twenty years, and went off, like the youngest son in fairy tales, to seek my fortune, and another different life. (pp. 146–147).

The entries after December tend to be reminiscences about people and events, comments on books she has read, and, toward the end of the journal, descriptions of the sights and sounds of her new community. There is less self-examination in the entries in the last third of the book, which is consistent with her March resolution to stop "clinging" to herself and to "look outward" (p. 206) and assume the posture of an observer of the drama around her. She describes negative events, such as unexpected repairs and the difficulty of packing all her books, but, unlike the entries for July and August, these events no longer reverberate with and reinforce a negative self-image.

A sure indication of Grumbach's changed state of mind is an entry in the last section of the journal on women who undertook new projects late in life, such as those described in Goldman's *Late Bloomer* interviews (Goldman, 1988). Grumbach's exemplars are Zelda Fitzgerald, who began ballet dancing well into her thirties, Edith Hamilton, who began to write her books on mythology after being forced to retire from her job as headmistress of the Bryn Mawr school, and Harriet Doerr, who published her first novel in her early seventies. Like the women she cites, she now, with some remaining hesitancy, writes that she, too, has a purpose for living: "I have work still to do, I think" (p. 238). In this phrase she affirms an intention to continue productive activity and in so doing tacitly expresses a faith in the value of that work. But the concluding two words "I think" reflect the doubts that still linger. This entry with its paean to the possibility of beginning successful new enterprises late in life stands in sharp contrast with an entry from July in which she is scornful about the idea of 70 being young these days (p. 58). At that point, it is likely she would have rejected the idea of new beginnings for older people as sentimental drivel.

By the time she reaches her 71st birthday, the despair of the first part of the book has been replaced by acceptance of her age and physical condition and hope for continued accomplishment.

> No longer am I burdened by the weight of my years. . . . I seem not to have grown older in the year, but more content with whatever age it is I am. . . . There may well be the enduring challenge of the 365 steps up the face of the Temple of the Dwarf at Chichén Itzá, but the certainty that I shall never again climb them no longer disturbs me. . . . I've begun to try to turn up the lights on what remains of my life. . . . I am ready to begin the end. (pp. 251–252)

The image of turning up the lights on the rest of her life, derived from the reputed last words of O. Henry ("Turn up the lights—I don't want to go home in the dark"), aptly expresses her changed outlook. She has made an internal accommodation to the physical losses of aging and has renewed her commitment to work and to life.

Refining the Life Structure

When we speak of people as being refined, we usually mean they are elegant or polished. A different sense of the idea of refinement, however, occurs in the accounts of aging found in personal journals in general and particularly in Grumbach's journal. Refinement also means the process of becoming free of impurities and of moving toward a pure state. This is the sense in which the word is being used here in relation to Grumbach's (and other journal writers') descriptions of the feeling of stripping away unnecessary obligations, discarding objects that had once been desired and required but that have now become burdens, and living a life in which the urgings of the self form the ground of day-to-day activity.

The idea of refining the self is expressed by Grumbach most directly in a January entry in which she states "I will do noth-

ing in my life that I do not want to do. Nothing. Ever again."
(p. 151). We do not have to take this as a statement of literal
truth, but rather as a policy intended to guide decisions about
future commitments. She is aware that this policy could be
viewed by others as unmitigated selfishness and comments
that she is in a new age of self-indulgence (p. 42). But what
lies behind the policy is not what is behind the egocentrism
of children or the narcissism of certain adults, but rather is a
consequence of the realistic appraisal of the limited amount
of time she has left to live. Within a narrowing time horizon,
every moment increases in value. Therefore it is critically
important not to waste time on what is no longer essential to
creating a sense of well-being.

The activity of determining what is essential is explicitly
addressed in several entries. Grumbach refers to this activity as "taking stock." She describes stock–taking as "looking
at what I had and have and was and am and did and do, what
I no longer wish to be and do and keep and acquire" (p. 59).
She asks herself questions: Is there anything of significance
I still wish to acquire? Is there anything I have that I no longer
wish to keep? Is it possible, at this late date, to lead a life based
on principles, a guiding philosophy? Do I take seriously as I
should the fact of my mortality? (pp. 68–69).

For Grumbach, avoiding the inessential means getting rid
of many belongings that have been accumulated over the
years, including many of books. For a person whose life is
books and who is personally acquainted with the authors of
many books she owns, this is a painful process. The move to
Maine speeds up the discarding of no longer necessary objects, and turns the July resolution into an actuality.

Aside from material objects, certain ideas also serve as
components of the life structure. The process of refining the
life structure also means eliminating strictures we have placed
on ourselves over a lifetime, strictures that have outlived
whatever usefulness there may once have been. One such
stricture described by Grumbach is the idea that she must

finish reading every book she begins. She resolves to leave unfinished any book she does not like. Another set of ideas that can be held up for examination is what we hold as dreams and aspirations. Refinement of the life structure in part entails giving up dreams that will not materialize, a process that Levinson calls de-illusionment (Levinson et al., 1978, p. 192).

Thus, for Grumbach the process of refining the life structure involves eliminating certain ideas and many belongings. Interestingly, she experiences the elimination of the inessential as a shift in focus from the interior (me and mine) to the exterior. Even though her policy of not doing anything she does not want to do sounds like selfishness, the life she intends to lead will, she hopes, actually be less saturated with the self than her earlier life.

> It is time to stop clinging to myself and my "belongings," the foolish solipsism that I have always been guilty of, and begin to look outward. If there are to be some good years, I intend to take an elementary course in the moods and changes of Billings Cove, from early morning to the dying light, and then raise my eyes to an advanced study of Eggemoggin Reach beyond the cove, and after that do graduate work on the glory of the surrounding hills and woods. It may be that in this way I will empty my glutted interior self, and fill it with the beauty of a world that is not the self, and never has been. (pp. 206–207)

What is essential to the inner person comes to coincide with what is of enduring beauty in the outside world.

COMMENTARY

Erik Erikson identified Integrity versus Despair as the central developmental dilemma of later life. Erikson, a careful chooser of words, selected the term integrity to evoke the idea of wholeness and oneness coupled with the idea of adherence to principles. Integrity connotes a sense of the wholeness of life, the feeling that one's life makes sense, that there is an underlying unity to the whole story, and that there is value and meaning in one's life. (The importance of maintaining narrative coherence will be discussed further in Chapter 8.) Integrity also connotes the idea of living according to the principles one professes. The principles relevant to the lives of older people are the hard-won personal convictions about how life should be led and about what, ultimately, really matters.

The dilemma arises because with advancing age there are constant assaults on one's sense of integrity. One's sense of wholeness is partly built upon being rooted in a social world, in a geographic locale and in a body. The assaults to the sense of integrity arise from irreversible losses that aging brings in each of these domains. There are inevitable losses owing to the deaths of family members and lifetime friends; there are losses that arise because of changes in neighborhoods and deterioration of housing; and there are losses relating to the decline in the functioning of the body. The accumulation of such losses can lead to the feeling that Erikson labels as despair.

With each of Erikson's dilemmas the issues pertaining to the central developmental dilemma do not arise *de novo* at a particular chronological age. Each of the developmental dilemmas is assumed to be present at each chronological age. There is, however, presumed to be a developmental shift in the central or predominant issue. Thus, for school age children, the central issue is understood to be industry versus inferiority. This is not to say that the conflict between autonomy and shame and doubt is completely absent from the school age child's life. Rather, the earlier resolution of that issue is reworked at the later chronological age. Similarly, saying that the central developmental dilemma of school age children is industry versus inferiority does not mean that concern about generativity versus stagnation, the central developmental issue of middle adulthood, is absent from the school-age child's life. Clearly, school age children can, do, and should have concerns about taking care of others, the idea at the heart of Erikson's notion of generativity. According to the theory, all eight of the core developmental dilemmas are present throughout life. Each developmental dilemma is preworked and reworked with the passage of time.

McAdams (1988) uses the metaphor of stories in a newspaper to explain the idea of the continuing presence, but shifting importance, of Erikson's eight developmental dilemmas. McAdams asks us to imagine a newspaper with lead stories on its front page and stories of continuing but lesser importance on inside pages. Lead stories often stay front-page news for a period and then are moved to the back pages. Similarly, stories that start out on the back pages can, over a period of time, take on added significance and move to the front pages. Erikson's developmental dilemmas can be understood in this way. Each dilemma has a chronological period when it is most prominent. But even when it is not the lead story, it is still part of the news. There continue to be experiences that shape the person's resolution of that issue.

Thus, to say that integrity versus despair is the central developmental dilemma of late life is not to say that people cannot be challenged by the loss of meaning and purpose at earlier ages. To the contrary, according to Erikson's model, the possibility of despair accompanies us throughout life. It is, however, the focal issue of later life.

What is it like to be in a state of despair? The writings of existential psychotherapists are especially helpful for analyzing the components of this feeling. Yalom's (1980; 1989) discussion of the "givens" of existence, what might be termed the existential facts of life, provides a basis for developing an anatomy of despair. Yalom proposes four such facts: the inevitability of death for each of us and for those we love; the freedom to make our lives as we will; our ultimate aloneness; and the absence of any obvious meaning or sense to life. For Yalom, people typically seek psychotherapy because of paralyzing anxieties relating to one or more of these existential givens. The process of psychotherapy allows people to confront these facts and to develop responses to them that permit change and growth. However, the anxieties about the existential givens, which lead people to seek therapy, can also collectively be understood as the components of what Erikson termed despair.

Death is an obvious fact of life. At an early age, people learn that death will come and also develop ways of denying or escaping the reality of death. But it is one thing to know the facts intellectually and quite another to know them emotionally. Typically, people split off the terror-inducing feeling associated with death from the intellectual knowledge of death's reality. At times, however, the terror can break through, for example after a personal brush with death or when a loved one has died. It is useful to think of one component of despair as uncontrolled death anxiety.

The idea of freedom is generally viewed as unequivocally positive. However, our existential freedom means that each of us is, to a degree, the author of our choices, actions, and life situations. There is no genetically or societally determined structure or design to individual lives. Lives, or what Levinson (1978) would term life structures, are the sum of choices made and enacted. Yalom identifies two problems relating to groundlessness of human existence: identifying what one wants and deciding to act. Sometimes people are wish-blocked. From among the myriad of choices that life offers, they are unable to identify what they want. People also may be decision-blocked. They may be stymied by the hard reality that each decision eliminates options, entails renunciation of some desirable alternative. For every yes there must be a no (Levinson et al., 1978, p. 43; Yalom, 1989, p. 10). We can think of the feeling of the groundlessness of existence as a second component of despair.

A third existential fact of life is our ultimate aloneness, the unbridgeable gap between ourselves and others, a gap that exists even in the presence of deeply gratifying interpersonal relationships. "No matter how close each of us becomes to another, there remains a final unbridgeable gap; each of us enters existence alone and must depart from it alone" (Yalom, 1980, p. 9). Though our embeddedness in social groups typically masks this aloneness, there are times when the reality of aloneness breaks through. Especially when death approaches people may become painfully aware of their ultimate isolation. Yalom mentions hearing many dying patients say that the most awful thing about dying is that it must be done alone. Isolation can be viewed as a third component of despair

The final existential fact of life is that there is no given, necessary, or prescribed meaning to life. This is the sense that our life has (or, in the case of older people, has had) no purpose, that it makes no ultimate difference that we have lived. We are meaning-seeking creatures and, yet in reality there is no meaning out there for us to find. Being overwhelmed by the meaninglessness of life can be viewed as fourth component of despair.

People in despair have failed to develop or have lost their grip on successful strategies for responding to one or more of these four aspects of existence—strategies that allow for the possibility of happiness and a sense of integrity.

Grumbach's period of despair recorded at the beginning of the journal can be understood as a collapsing of defenses against each of the grim facts of life. The journal is especially valuable for expressing thoughts that accompany two of Yalom's existential givens, groundlessness and meaninglessness. During the dark months at the beginning of the journal, Grumbach expresses the idea that the existential grounding of her life has dissolved. Grumbach talks about her loss of faith and that what she had faith in had been removed, changed, or deleted. She repeatedly mentions trying and failing to find some philosophical basis for what she has been. The sense of groundlessness is intertwined with expressions of meaninglessness. She asks what her life has meant and cannot provide an answer. She asserts that at the end of life, the value of what we thought matters is lost to us and, approvingly, quotes Pound to the effect that nothing really matters at all.

We may ask whether Grumbach has really lost the grounding and meaning in her life. After all, she was still grounded enough in her beliefs and her sense of self to be keeping the journal. Are the expressions of groundlessness and meaninglessness just a pose for the journal? Is she exaggerating?

Although, as with any text, other readings are possible, there is a consistency to the entries that makes them credible as expressions of the author's actual feelings. Even if Grumbach never reached psychological nadirs encountered by psychotherapists in their work with suicidal clients, the journal is still highly valuable for the way it reveals a person on the edge of deep despair and the way it documents the recovery of hope.

Alan Olmstead and the Fashioning of Purpose   6

PROFILE

Alan Olmstead was editor of the Manchester, Connecticut, *Evening Herald* and was a frequent contributor to *The New Yorker*. His first book, *Europe As I Saw It* (1938), was about his experiences as a foreign correspondent in Europe in the 1930s. After the war, in addition to his work as editor of the Manchester paper, he wrote a political column for the Bridgeport, Connecticut, *Times Star* called "The Wailing Wall," and later wrote a column called "*The Connecticut Yankee*," which was published in several Connecticut newspapers. His book *Threshold: The First Days of Retirement*, the subject of this chapter, was published in 1975. This was followed in 1977 by a book containing his reflections on nature, *In Praise of Seasons*.

Olmstead was married and had three daughters. In 1972, he retired at age 65. His retirement was voluntary in the sense that he was not forced to retire on account of reaching a mandatory retirement age. Psychologically, however, it was involuntary in that differences with new owners of the paper led to an earlier retirement than he had anticipated. Olmstead died in 1980.

THE JOURNAL

Olmstead's journal covers the first six months of his life after retirement. It is a disciplined and sharply crafted work. There is an entry every day between Monday, September 4, 1972, and Wednesday, March 14, 1973. The entries are consistently 300–400 words long. Each entry has a title and is a reflection on a clearly focused idea. The entries are laced with wry humor and often build to a concluding sentence that flashes out at the reader like the punch line of a good story.

The fact that the entries are so carefully crafted does not mean that they are any less personal or revealing. To the contrary, the journal is like a guided tour of an interior terrain. It is as if Olmstead is saying: "OK folks, here's what you'll encounter on the first part of your trip. . . . Don't forget to watch out for those dangerous feelings on the left. . . . After a while you'll begin to have this other thought."

Despite the diversity of attractions along the way, there are themes that are repeatedly articulated and which, through their repetition, illuminate the sense of what it means to retire in a way no questionnaire survey of retirees can match. Most prominent among these themes are the need for purpose and discipline, changes in reflective self-awareness, time and aging, retirement and marriage, and concerns about money.

Fashioning Purpose and Establishing Discipline

Five months into retirement, during a mid-February emotional low, Olmstead described the presence outside his study window of a blighted elm which had been entangled by a bittersweet vine. He related how the battle between the tree and the vine had been going on for years. The preceding year the tree finally succumbed, not to the vine, but to Dutch elm disease. It then put out a last birth of leaves and died in midsummer. Olmstead wrote that the vine, "acting as if it, the coiled assailant and not any invisible blight, had been responsible for some kind of victory over the elm, flowered and berried itself into a solidly massed crown." He goes on as follows:

> Now, for a few years to come, the vine which has just developed its full vigor is going to be tightening its coiled grip on the elm while the elm, no longer able to renew itself, must gradually, inevitably decay, perhaps to the point where the vine is . . . holding up the tree. I feel inside, like the old tree, never destined to be very tall and now forbidden to grow any more, while all the late-flowering parasitic ambitions of my pensioner imagination are making a sudden effort to overcome, hide, and yet still pinion themselves to the interior disintegration which is surely taking place. One day the elm will come down, porous and crumbled. Meanwhile, it feels good still to be gripped, firmly, by something, even late flowering dreams. (p. 184)

The image of the tree being gripped by the bittersweet vine captures a theme which is repeated throughout the journal: the necessity for retirees to deliberately fashion routines, disciplines, and, ultimately, purposes for living in order to be "gripped, firmly, by something." One of Olmstead's early postretirement discoveries is that there is nothing out there in the world that really depends on him, nothing externally imposed, nothing he really has to do. This is in sharp contrast to his preretirement life, in which there were many obligations, most notably the obligation to produce daily instant judgments about current events for the editorial page of his paper. Olmstead is very clear about the way such responsibilities structure time, give purpose to life, and provide self esteem. After having lunch with work friends, he writes that he had the feeling that his companions had a "traction and momentum and direction" (p. 121) in their lives that he in his new existence lacked.

The dissolving of work-role obligations not only creates the challenge of what to do with one's time but also raises the question of why one should do anything. Olmstead characterizes this as the "lazy siren lure of just to be without doing anything" (p. 23). This idea has a cancer-like quality. It can spread and turn into the devaluation of earlier purposes. At one point Olmstead writes:

> I am beginning to think it would never have made any difference if my particular factory [his newspaper] had not been operating at all. Neither what I produced there, in the course of a lifetime, nor what any successors may produce there has really mattered or will matter to anybody. (p. 181)

A deliberate act of will is required to escape from such thoughts. With the loss of externally imposed demands on his time, Olmstead becomes aware of the need for self-imposed routines and disciplines. The justification for these routines lies entirely within the person. You cannot depend on the results of any set of activities making a difference to anybody but yourself. Olmstead showers every day because he has to live with himself, not because he might be "potentially odorant" to anybody. He wears a tie every day. He organizes his study and his papers. And he recognizes that there is a delicate mental posture that must be adopted in relation to such self-imposed routines. "You must never let yourself stop to ask if it really makes any difference whether or not, for instance, you get up at the same time every retirement morning. . . . What may be hard to prove in relation to any particular morning is self-evident in the long range sense" (p. 98). Self-imposed routines also, interestingly, create the possibility of leisure. For nonretirees, the notion that retirees might not always have leisure time is paradoxical. Retirement, it is assumed, is full-time leisure. Olmstead makes it clear that this is a misunderstanding. The retiree's self-imposed routines and disciplines provide a "context of chore or obligation."

They are "bread for the leisure sandwich." Leisure, freedom from obligations, can only exist in relation to obligations. To preserve the experience of leisure, the experience of obligation must also be preserved.

Changes in Reflective Self Awareness

One feature of human cognition is that people not only have ideas about their own characteristics but they also have ideas about what others think of them, ideas that may be accurate or inaccurate but nonetheless exist and powerfully influence behavior. This human capacity for reflective self-awareness has long been the basis of theorizing in psychology, going back certainly at least as far as Cooley's idea of the looking-glass self. It is an idea that plays a prominent role in conceptualizations of interpersonal perception (Laing, 1966) and in social psychological research on social comparison theory (Suls & Wills, 1991). Olmstead's deliberations about what others think of him raise the interesting possibility that aging creates the potential for increasing the accuracy of our judgments of others' perceptions of us.

In various entries, Olmstead recalls feelings he had about older people when he was younger. In an entry similar to one in Vining's journal discussed previously, he realizes he is now the age which he had previously pitied and scorned. Commenting on a luncheon outing to a restaurant with his wife, he notes:

> [W]e were behaving exactly in the style of some of the well-known retired couples about town we used to watch with a mixture of admiration, wonder, and pity. We used to admire the way they kept up their immaculate appearance. We used to wonder how much forced and anguished pretense might go into their public masquerade of contentment and security. We used to pity them for the possibility that what really kept them on the move for such unimportant errands and time-killers was some cruel experience of loneliness and boredom. (p. 128)

In this passage Olmstead is recalling his reactions to a certain type of older couple—the type that he and his wife now exemplify. He and his wife probably do evoke exactly the same thoughts of "admiration, wonder and pity" in those who are now the age he was in the past. He knows what they are thinking because he thought so himself in the past. Now that he is older, he is in a position to report that those who currently hold the ideas he held when he was younger are off the mark. "We need no sympathy and require no pity" (p. 129). The outing that he and his wife had was not prompted by loneliness or boredom. Rather its basis was that it is possible for "two people, who have long ago established their mutual assurances, to have a good time doing rather inconsequential things together" and that there are "routines that have a mellow richness all their own" (p. 129).

Other such instances of sharpened awareness of others' perceptions of him are prompted by contemplating a visit to his old office and by conversations with younger people. He does not actually visit his old office because of recollecting what such visits were like.

> I don't believe there ever was an instance of a retired employee just dropping in to see how things were going that didn't set off a time clock ticking inside everybody, measuring, sometimes with patience, but sometimes with increasingly obvious gestures toward some piece of work waiting to be done, just how long this interruption was going to last. (p. 197)

Olmstead anticipates how he would be viewed by others because he, himself, occupied the position of the other in the past. Similarly, he knows what happens when old people and young people have conversations and how young people are turned off by the "pushy frequency" of the tales of the old. Olmstead anticipates what would happen if he were to say "I remember when" or "when I first went to work" based on what his responses were in similar situations when he was a younger listener. Now that he is older, he hopes he can avoid being perceived as a garrulous old man and sets up rules for reminiscing. His first rule for reminiscence is "Don't." He adds, though, that this is not an absolute don't. His second rule covers the kind of reminiscing older people should produce when asked about the old days. "Train yourself," he writes, "to go to one concrete and briefly phrased response, presented without embroidery and so shaped that unless somebody persists in asking another question or imploring amplification, what you say in this first response will wrap the reminiscence up and leave the conversation free to veer where everybody else may please." He suggests this will have a highly desirable effect: "You will begin to gain a reputation that will be dear to your ego—that you are not like other oldsters, not at all" (pp. 149–150).

Time and Aging

Aging brings about a change in a person's relationship with time. One aspect of this change, previously mentioned in the discussion of Doris Grumbach's diary, is the time perspective shift that begins at mid-life, originally described by Neugarten (1968). The shift in time perspective involves a reorientation from how much time has elapsed since birth to how much time is remaining. The reorientation entails a change in the psychological significance of chronological age. Chronological age becomes associated with thoughts of the limited number of years that remain and what can realistically be accomplished in those years. Such an orientation to time is in contrast to the orientation that dominates childhood, when chronological age is associated with increasing capacity rather than decreasing opportunity. An example of a child's perspective on the significance of chronological age would be the declaration by a four-year-old that three-year-olds cannot climb to the top of the monkey bars. Greater distance from birth is associated with increased capacity. Examples of older adults' perspectives on the psychological significance of chronological age are a 55-year-old woman's feeling that she probably has only one or two more career moves remaining until retirement or an 80-year-old man's feeling that he probably only has a few years remaining until his death.

These tendencies should be thought of as predominant modes of experiencing rather than clearly demarcated, mutually exclusive stages. On occasion, older people can adopt the time perspective that predominates in childhood and feel their capacities are currently greater than they were in the past. They can focus on the way their capacities, especially the capacity to make judgments about difficult and uncertain matters of life, have increased. The studies of Baltes and his colleagues show how cognitive capacities related to this form of judgment, which they label as wisdom, do, indeed, have the potential to increase with increasing age (Baltes, Smith, Staudinger, & Sowarka, 1990). Similarly, younger people can, like older people, feel that time is running out and focus on how little time remains. A. E. Housman's poem "Loveliest of Trees" expresses the feeling of a 20-year-old that even the 50 more years of life remaining to him according to the biblical allotment would be too little to appreciate the brief annual magnificent spring display of cherry blossoms.[1] However, despite the possibility of such reversals, the predomi-

---

[1]Loveliest of trees, the cherry now
Is hung with bloom along the bough,
And stands about the woodland ride
Wearing white for Eastertide.

Now, of my threescore years and ten,
Twenty will not come again,
And take from seventy springs a score,
It only leaves me fifty more.

And since to look at things in bloom
Fifty springs are little room,
About the woodlands I will go
To see the cherry hung with snow.
(A. E. Housman, 1965)

nant orientation of the young is "time since birth" and after mid-life "time remaining."

Olmstead has his own incisive and humorous way of expressing the shift in time perspective. In an entry titled "The Big Deadline," he describes how before retirement life is full of small deadlines that constantly have to be met. After retirement, though, all the little deadlines have faded and are replaced by one big new deadline, "Something like the sudden-death period in sports when every play or stroke may be the last, the one that determines the final score of the whole long game" (p. 14). There is, he writes, only so much time left for *everything*:

> Where there were once various enterprises that needed to be completed on schedule, the new big deadline is one against which all one's life must necessarily be completed. None of the petty exigencies matters much any more. But what one really wants to do before the big deadline arrives—that is what is urgently important to find out, and to do if one can. (p. 14)

The big deadline is responsible for feeling busy and rushed:

> No wonder I feel, at that very stage of life when they say one is supposed and entitled to take it easy, as if I had never been in such a frantic hurry, with so many things to do in such cruelly little time. (p. 126)

Along with feeling in a frantic hurry there is the sense that time is passing quickly. On February 20, he sees the first blackbird of spring and comments that the advent of spring is too early for his state of mind. In September he wondered if he would make it to spring through the first months of retirement. Now spring has arrived: "[T]his perhaps over-anticipated period of test and challenge is receding behind me before I have even managed to experience it very deeply" (pp. 188–189). Nor has he accomplished all that he hoped to accomplish.

Olmstead also describes another difference that retirement has brought about in his experience of time, a difference that is in a certain respect opposite to the frantic hurry imposed by the Big Deadline. Despite awareness of the Big Deadline, the relative freedom from externally imposed obligations means that retirees are not locked into the schedules of those in the working world. Retirees, Olmstead notes, are exempted from the urgency of getting someplace or getting home by any certain hour. This means they can, among other things, eat in fancy restaurants at off hours—which sacrifices only the time of day and provides luxury at half the price. Retirees move in their own time zone and are not to be pitied by the more purposeful travelers of the world (p. 159).

Retirement and Marriage

There is another person present in many entries in the journal, Olmstead's wife, Catherine, whom he refers to as C. The nature of their relationship is revealed in the journal and several entries address the impact of retirement on that relationship. Naturally, the impact of retirement on a marital relationship depends on what that relationship was like to begin with. Olmstead and C have had a long marriage of the traditional type: he has worked in the office and she has worked in the home. Moreover, the division of responsibility when he was not at the office was also traditional. For example, in the journal he indicates that he does not vacuum (in fact, resents her vacuuming) and until retirement had not helped dry the dishes.

Readers of the journal, both male and female, who have more egalitarian marriages will undoubtedly bristle at the fuss Olmstead makes over the thought of helping to dry the dishes: "Since I no longer go out and drudge all day in an office in order to bring home the bacon, perhaps it has now come time for me to lighten the work load C has been carrying at home all these years" (p. 35). He goes on to examine the question of whether he should begin going to the kitchen after supper rather than to the television. The next day after dinner, he makes an impulsive decision, goes to the kitchen, ostentatiously grabs a towel, then a dish. His wife does not, contrary to his expectations, say she wants to do the dishes by herself, but rather warns him that the dishes will be real hot. He concludes the entry as follows:

> Tonight, being there at her side felt better than being in with the television. But I must try to discipline myself. It doesn't have to be a regular thing. (p. 37)

The journal illustrates how in a marriage built around the traditional division of role activities, there can still be companionship and deep affection. This is most apparent in Olmstead's discussions of activities he shares with C: gardening, reading poetry, working the tree farm, taking excursions to restaurants, and riding around the countryside. The happiness he expresses in these shared activities and the love he expresses for C's mere presence outweigh the reservations we might have about what he calls his innocent chauvinism.

He knows, though, that retirement can create problems for marriages. He recognizes that his wife has been asked a number of times "What's it like having him around the house?" though he doesn't know how she responds. And he knows that putting two people in the same living space every day creates tension. Two occasions are recorded when his wife was cross with him (though none when he was cross with her). There are two points about her habitual behavior that trouble Olmstead and relate to the situation of retiring husbands in traditional marriages. The first is the telephone. Olmstead describes how he has established a rule that when the telephone rings, he always waits for C to answer it. With a considerable measure of self-mockery, he explains the reasons for the rule:

1. I don't have to explain to people who ought to know anyway why I am at home and not working any more.
2. I don't have to make up amiable chit-chat for people who just want to talk to C.
3. I don't have to keep needlessly invading C's privacy. I can ask her, after she has hung up, who it was and what he or she wanted.
4. I achieve an atmosphere of aloofness and importance, as if C were my secretary. (p. 33)

The problem with this arrangement is that in the first days of his retirement there were three calls for him for every one for her. He needed to be near the phone. After a month, however, calls for him have all but ended and calls for his wife have returned to the level where they were before he was home all day: "[H]er friends, playing it cool and aloof in the first days they knew I might be around the house, were relaxing again, and she with them" (p. 34). His wife, of course, had not retired. Her life, particularly her life with her friends, continued on as before. And, to a certain extent, Olmstead is jealous. He does not want her not to talk on the telephone, but because he is in the house, he is aware of how much she is on the telephone with her friends in a way that he wasn't when he was working. He is aware, in effect, of how much more she is connected with and needed by the outside world than he is.

A similar sore point exists in connection with his wife's outings with friends. He records several occasions when his wife goes out with friends to visit a garden, to shop, or to have lunch. These were, presumably, a regular part of her life before he retired. His retirement has not ended these activities. But he misses her even though he knows that the "good life together depends on occasional divergences of activity" (p. 35).

Despite the emotional jostling of being together almost all the time and Olmstead's ambivalence about times when his wife is on the telephone or away, the overall message about retirement and this marriage is one of continuity and happiness. It is clear that retirement has enabled him and his wife to do more of what they like to do together, "the routines that have a mellow richness all their own," referred to earlier, and he says that he and his wife have never found more pleasure in each other's presence.

Concerns about Money

There is a subjective side to the economics of aging which is more difficult to assess than the actual dollars available to retirees but is, nonetheless, a significant part of the retirement experience.

Olmstead is a member of the group of retirees who experience a sharp decline in income after retirement. In an entry called Retirement Arithmetic, he gives the details of his financial situation. His assets are quite limited, even in terms of 1972 dollars: $6,800 in savings, $4,000 in stocks, the value of his property and house. His monthly income will be derived from Social Security and a small pension from the newspaper. His post-retirement income will be approximately 50% of his preretirement income. Although retirees do not need to replace 100% of their preretirement income to maintain their standard of living (Schulz, 1992), Olmstead's fifty percent decline in income means that maintaining his preretirement standard of living will be difficult. It is not surprising, therefore, that concerns about money constitute a daily issue in the Olmstead home and are a frequent topic in the journal. The journal makes clear the way that this concern pervades the activities of the many people who are in the Olmsteads' situation. One point made clear in the journal is that people who are retired have the time to be frugal. They can economize by shopping for bargains and eating out at lunch time rather than dinner. Working people cannot do this. Furthermore, the motive of saving money helps organize their day and provides a purpose for a set of activities.

Concerns about money are also a significant feature of dealing with other people. Olmstead reflects on the way that he and his wife intend to appear to others just as well off as they ever were, trying to dress as well as ever and go to the theater more, not less, often. They will, however, be poor in private, which he thinks is "no pain." His public posture of being as well off as ever is strained, however, by the constant requests for charitable donations: telephone solicitations, door-to-door canvassers, alumni funds, testimonial dinners. Such solicitations often start with what for the new retiree is the embarrassing line: "Last year you gave fifty dollars. Are you planning to match it or can we hope for a little more?" Interestingly, Olmstead advises not saying no to all these requests. They represent ties to the outside world. "Life—being and feeling a part of life—is still the number one necessity" (p. 82).

There are idiosyncratic aspects of Olmstead's feelings about money relating to his experiences while growing up. He tells how when he was a student at Yale, he was taken by a banker who was a scholarship fund trustee down into a bank vault and was made to hold a million dollars in thousand-dollar bills. He believes this experience left him not with a desire to accumulate money, which was the banker's intention, but rather with nervousness and unhappiness about the accumulation of money. Elsewhere, he talks about his lifelong talent for not making money and his uncertainty about handling the sale of Christmas trees from the tree farm he and his wife had started years before. Also, the fact that, according to his own account, he and his wife had not started saving for retirement until he was 63 further confirms that money was a chronic problem for this man.

But one aspect of Olmstead's feelings about money that is likely not to be idiosyncratic but rather quite common among retiring men of his generation is described in the entry entitled "Is Social Security Manly?" The occasion for the entry is the arrival of the first Social Security check. Olmstead remembers the beginning of Social Security under Roosevelt and bitterly recalls the way that employees were told that it was a scheme to defraud the workers. He views his Social Security check as a wonderful thing—a guarantee that he will not starve. He recognizes that he has been paying into Social Security since 1937 and that he certainly deserves this money. But he is uncomfortable nonetheless. He asks whether, in accepting his first Social Security check, he is implicitly sealing some kind of a bargain, unintentionally giving over something *more* than 35 years of payroll deductions in exchange for financial security. He wonders whether he is a ward of the state or something less of a success as a man to be needing this kind of help. "Although I may find logic which says that my manhood has not been in any way diminished, the feeling that something left my life when these checks came into it will still persist" (pp. 64–65).

COMMENTARY

Constructing Existential Meaning

Human science identifies meaning-making as the central activity of human beings. As Kegan (1982) has succinctly written, "the activity of being a person is the activity of meaning-making" (p. 11). But there is a seminal ambiguity in the term meaning-making. It refers to two different activities. In one sense, we may speak of meaning-making as the moment-to-moment transformation of the flow of experience into language. This sense of meaning-making involves the interpretation of sensory inputs and the development of tacit, logically consistent, prediction-oriented theories. Human beings constantly create meaning (in this sense of the term) by observing the behavior and listening to the speech of other human beings. Fingarette (1963) uses the term *scientific* to designate this aspect of meaning-making. Implicit in his use of that adjective is the metaphor of people as scientists, who make inferences about meaning based on interpretive schemata.

Meaning-making in this sense is the central feature of several major research traditions, most notably Kelly's personal construct psychology, Piaget's genetic epistemology, and attribution theory in social psychology.

A second sense of meaning-making can be designated *existential*. It pertains to the answers a person provides to questions about life's meaning or meaninglessness. This second sense of meaning-making is typically what is intended in the phrase "the search for meaning," the clinical implications of which have been explored by Maddi (1970) and Frankl (1963; 1969; 1971; 1978). Yalom (1980, p. 419) presents some of the forms taken by questions of existential meaning: What is the meaning of life? What is the meaning of *my* life? Why do we live? Why were we put here? What do we live for? What shall we live by? If we must die, if nothing endures, then what sense does anything make?

Yalom also points out that it is possible to distinguish between questions of meaning and questions of purpose. Strictly speaking, meaning refers to what gives coherence to life, whereas purpose refers to aims or goals of life. But conventional usage treats them synonymously and speaks interchangeably of the meaning or purpose of life.

Although there have been many empirical investigations of the scientific aspect of meaning-making, empirical investigation of existential meaning-making has been quite limited. However, Reker and Wong (1988) have made an admirable effort at charting a program of empirical investigation into existential meaning. Because of the relevance of their work to the kind of issues people take up in personal diaries and the ambition of Reker and Wong's enterprise, it is worthwhile to consider their essay in detail.

The program of research they describe consists of a description of metatheoretical framework, a conceptualization of what they term personal meaning, a set of measurement instruments appropriate to their conceptualization, and an initial set of testable hypotheses. Drawing on the term used by

Rabinow and Sullivan (1979; 1987), they identify their meta-theoretical framework as the interpretive social science perspective. The assumptions of this metatheory, according to Reker and Wong are, first, that human beings are conscious, active, purposive, self-reflecting organisms capable of symbolization and symbol manipulation; and second, that personal meanings attached to objects and events are more significant realities for investigation than the physical attributes of the natural world. In this second assumption, Reker and Wong seem to be referring to the scientific, rather than the existential sense of meaning-making; yet, as will become apparent, their program of research is clearly oriented toward the investigation of existential meaning.

Reker and Wong's conceptualization of personal meaning is derived principally from the writings of Frankl and Maddi. Following Maddi, they characterize personal meaning as having cognitive, motivational, and affective components. Personal meaning is the cognizance of order, coherence and purpose; the pursuit and attainment of worthwhile goals; and the accompanying sense of fulfillment. Despite numerous references in their essay to the creation of personal meaning being an individual process and statements about the importance of idiographic research, the approach to the study of personal meaning that they elaborate heavily emphasizes presentation of postulates and hypotheses pertaining to interindividual differences in personal meaning.

Reker and Wong propose that personal meaning varies in degree. In other words, they implicitly suggest that individuals differ in the degree to which their lives are meaningful. The degree of personal meaning is postulated to vary according to the breadth of the sources (e.g., leisure activities, creative abilities, personal relationships, religious beliefs, etc.) and the level of the values (e.g., meeting basic needs versus service to others) to which an individual is committed. The combination of breadth and depth produces meaning system complexity. More complexity implies a higher degree of differentiation and integration. Personal meanings also vary in terms of the context from which they are created. Context is defined as varying along a unidimensional continuum anchored by poles of social versus self-definitions of meaning. Social definitions of personal meaning are those which are created from societal expectations; self-definitions are those in which the boundaries of social expectations are transcended and the individual is emancipated from the past. Following Maddi, they label those who create meaning from societal expectations as conformists and those who create meaning from self-definitions as individualists. Reker and Wong hypothesize that the personal meaning systems of individualists are more differentiated and integrated than those of people who conform to cultural prescriptions.

Reker and Wong's approach also includes measurement tools for assessing meaning system breadth, level, and complexity, as well as an instrument to measure the strength of motivation to find personal meaning in life. They also acknowledge the importance of qualitative approaches to complement their elaborate list of quantitative measures, but they do not indicate how qualitative information would be integrated with their quantitative measures.

The results of investigations that would follow from the model Reker and Wong present remain to be seen. At this point what they have presented is a program of research based on a thoughtful analysis of existential meaning. It is appropriate, however, to consider the assumptions underlying this model. Does the model itself adequately reflect the character of existential meaning-making?

One troubling aspect of the model is the discussion of personal meaning contexts. As noted, Reker and Wong propose that there is a meaning-producing continuum. Individuals are presumed to vary in the extent to which they abide by societal expectations, sticking close to norms, versus transcending the boundaries of social expectations. Reker and Wong postulate that an individual chooses a position on the meaning producing continuum and hypothesize that the personal meaning system of the individualist is more differentiated and integrated, (i.e., better) than that of the conformist. In developing this argument, Reker and Wong (and Maddi from whom they drew the idea) echo the individualist orientation of Western society discussed in Chapter 2. In this view individualism is good and conformity is bad.

As discussed in Chapter 2, the Western penchant to view being an individual as good and conforming to a group as bad has been critiqued from a variety of perspectives. What is most relevant here about the assumption that individualists have better meaning systems than conformists is that it oversimplifies the dynamic interplay between conformity and individuality in creating existential meaning. To understand this interplay, it is helpful to return to arguments developed by Becker, which were introduced in Chapter 4 and will be developed further here.

Transference Heroics

According to Becker, to be human is to be poised between two opposing fears, the fear of life and the fear of death. The fear of life arises from the realization of the powerlessness and insignificance of human beings in relation to the vastness and arbitrariness of the universe. The reflex-like response to (i.e., the defense against) the fear of life is the urge to seek protection by becoming part of something larger and more powerful than oneself. However, human beings are also aware of and fear death. The reflex-like response to the fear of death is to try to transcend death. Efforts to transcend death can be viewed as attempts to achieve immortality, as ways of outliving the self (Kotre, 1984). Such efforts may involve striving to do something that matters and will be noticed and remembered or leaving something for the next generation.

Responding to the fear of death entails actions that move a person outward into the world and make a person "individual," that is, separate from others. Responding to the fear of life entails actions that lead to attachment, toward being encompassed by a larger entity, and, therefore, toward conforming to that larger entity. "[M]an wants the impossible: He wants to lose his isolation and keep it at the same time. He can't stand the sense of separateness, and yet he can't allow the complete suffocating of his vitality" (Becker, 1973, p. 155). The human situation is to be constantly pulled between the fear of life and the fear of death, the tendencies toward attachment and separateness.

This dilemma can be resolved through a relationship with a transference object. Transference, as Freud identified it, is a form of projection in which defenses developed by patients in dealing with significant others ("love objects") outside the therapeutic relationship are employed in the relationship with the therapist. The origins of such defensive patterns lie in people's earliest relationships with caregivers. In childhood, caregivers, typically mothers and fathers, are experienced by children as being omnipotent. Becker develops the idea of transference by focusing on the transference object as something outside the child that enables him or her to overcome smallness, unimportance, and vulnerability. By conforming to the dictates of the transference object, the child is protected. In this way, safe belongingness is assured and the fear of life is assuaged. But within the transference relationship, the child can attempt to excel, to become extra-special, to become unique, to develop what Becker terms the heroic gift and, thus, to assuage the fear of death. For the child, the meaning of life is fashioned within the context of early relationships with love objects. Relationships with love objects not only provide security but also establish the terms on which a person can do something that matters. As development continues beyond childhood, the transference object, that which encompasses the self and establishes the nature of the heroic gift, expands.

It comes to include childhood peer groups, teachers, societal institutions, reference groups, societal norms and religious creeds. In other words, transference relationships may be with abstract entities rather than particular others. Becker's argument is that the central feature of the dynamic relationship with transference objects established in childhood continues throughout life. Irrespective of how concrete or abstract the transference object is, we achieve a sense of security, freedom from the fear of life, through a psychological merger with it, while simultaneously transcending the fear of death by satisfying the transference object's dictates regarding what it takes to stand out, to be "outstanding," and what constitutes a proper legacy of self.

As adults, people are free to choose transference objects but often feel "unfree," sensing rather that they are bound by transference relationships established early in life. For most adults, transference objects are given by cultural definitions: the boss, the leader, the rules of society. They try to be good parents, good providers, or solid citizens. A sense of the meaning and purpose of life is achieved in an unreflective, automatic manner through conformity and surrender to what is nearest at hand. They give the heroic gift that society specifies in advance. Their transcendence of death is achieved through species immortality, by being an agent of procreation, or collective or cultural immortality, by perpetuating the norms of an immediately present social group. These are people Maddi would refer to as conformists.

Others take the issue of transference objects as a problem. They cannot accept collective at-hand solutions to resolving the opposing pulls of the fears of life and death. They invest themselves in transference relationships with more encompassing, more challenging transference objects. Such an orientation to life is characteristic of artists but also typifies others who derive meaning from what Reker and Wong term higher-level values. These are the people Maddi calls individualists.

It is important to recognize that regardless of the type of transference object selected, that is, regardless of what the person takes as the source of his or her life's meaning and purpose, the transference object is the locus of conscience. It is the authority that must be obeyed. It is a reality *beyond* the self that creates the basis for self-criticism and self-idealization. Even those who have established for themselves individualistic transference objects relate to those objects submissively. People choose transference objects and then submit to the dictates of those choices. "Even the strongest person . . . has to lay the burden of his life somewhere beyond him" (Becker, 1973, p. 250). In this sense, everyone is a conformist: we all submit to the dictates laid down by the transference objects we have chosen.

It is also important to recognize that even individualistic transference objects are given by society. Individualistic transference objects are not created *ex nihilo*. People who question whether their lives should be led according to the standards employed by those around them do that questioning using available categories of thought. New transference objects are fashioned from culturally (and linguistically) available structures of meaning, which are also societal givens, although they may not be adopted by the majority of people in society. Such structures of meaning constitute the categories in which more expansive purposes for living can be fashioned.

Reker and Wong's formulation captures the idea that there are different beyonds into which people strive to expand and that these beyonds vary in the extent to which they rest on at-hand or more abstract sources of meaning. However, the static nature of the model precludes analysis of the dynamics of existential meaning-making, particularly in regard to the way that individualism and conformity are intertwined in fashioning the meaning of one's life. The model also leads us to overlook the way that even the most individualistic meanings are derived from culturally available terms of discourse.

Olmstead Revisited

Olmstead's journal speaks to the existential side of meaning-making. Under its jocular surface are the deepest of questions: *What is the purpose of living? What is the meaning of my life?* In urging retirees to construct routines, disciplines, and purposes for living Olmstead is articulating a constructivist perspective. Meanings are not given or preestablished. Individuals construct their purposes, choose their transference objects.

It seems likely that for many people during most of adult life, the answers to the existential questions are arrived at by submitting to (in Becker's sense of choosing a transference object) societally given norms in the domains of work and family. That is, answers to questions like "What is the purpose of living?" are implicitly articulated in the ready-to-hand activities of making a living and nurturing a family. Regardless of however else we may characterize them, work and family are meaning-making domains. They establish meaning structures within which psychological rewards are achieved or lost. They establish the terms in which meaning can be created. What is not typically apparent is the "chosen-ness" of activities relating to work and family. We would not *have* to engage in these activities—in the overall scheme of things what difference does it make if we do or we don't? Rather, we choose to engage in them, but experience those choices as responses to externally imposed requirements. As Yalom (1980) observes,

> We are uncomfortable in the absence of meaning. Yet the purpose one creates does not relieve discomfort effectively if one continues to remember that one forged it. It is far more comforting to believe that the meaning is out there. (p. 463)

However, the realization that all purposes are chosen may surface in consciousness during the period in which people make the transition into retirement, a phase of life in which earlier purposes for living provided by the formal work role no longer apply because of the cessation of that role. Olmstead's journal expresses the idea that in the absence of traditionally available purposes for living new ones must be fashioned.

Most retirees are able to fashion new purposes for living despite the loss of a previously available domain of meaning-making. This is evident from the research which has documented that identity crisis (which in light of the preceding discussion could also be termed existential crisis) is *not* a typical consequence of retirement (Atchley, 1971; 1989). It probably is fair to say, however, that although retirement does not typically lead to existential crisis, it does pose an existential challenge. In this regard, retirement resembles other life disruptions that lead to the termination of rewards for adherence to traditional practices and thereby result in the surfacing of questions about the meaning and purpose of living (Yalom, 1980, p. 454).

Olmstead's metaphor of the disintegrating tree being held up by the flowering vine relates well to Becker's insights about transference heroics and Yalom's comment (cited above) about finding meaning "out there." The vine, which surrounds the disintegrating tree, grips it and holds it up. Analogously, the purposes that retirees themselves—and, indeed, people of any age—create are often *experienced* as external requirements that hold life in their grip. Once fashioned, it is as if purposes exist outside of the people who choose them. They take on a life and power of their own. The experience is that of being held or, as Olmstead says, "gripped" by something outside of oneself. Without such meanings and purposes we would surely fall.

In this chapter we have followed the idea of the fashioning of purpose, a central theme in Olmstead's journal, into a series of reflections on personal meaning. We questioned just how personal, that is, individual or unique, personal meaning can really be, and presented the idea of the dynamic interplay of conformity and individuality in the creation of personal meaning. The journal considered in the next chapter provides an opportunity to continue our reflections on the tension between conformity and individuality.

Florida Scott-Maxwell: Individuation in the Face of Frailty

7

One of the most powerful personal journals of later life is *The Measure of My Days*, by Florida Scott-Maxwell. This book is distinguished from the other journals considered here in that the author is both older (i.e., in her 80s, rather than 60s or 70s) and frailer than the other writers (except for Sarton in her last two journals). Consequently, her journal is especially valuable for revealing what inner life can be like when coupled with a failing body. The power of the book also lies in the clear articulation of its principal theme: the importance of being an individual and living out one's fate. From varying angles, this theme is approached again and again in the journal, each time expressed in strong language with repeated use of words like *passion, combat, greatness, and heroism.*

PROFILE

Schleuter and Schleuter's *Encyclopedia of British Women Writers* (1988) is the best source of biographical information on Florida Scott-Maxwell. Scott-Maxwell was born September 24, 1883, in Orange Park, Florida, and was raised by her father's family in Pittsburgh, Pennsylvania. She attended public schools from the ages of 10–13, then went to art school, and trained at a drama school in New York City. At 16, she began a career as a player of minor roles in a New York theater company. She also began writing short stories that were published in *Harper's* and *Century* magazines, and she became the first woman staff member of the *New York Evening Sun*, writing a weekly column.

In 1910, at age 27, she married Scott John Scott-Maxwell and left the U.S. to live with him in his native Scotland. For 16 years, she lived in Ballieston house, near Glasgow, bearing four children and working for women's suffrage. During this time, she published a feminist play, *The Flash Point* (1914). She divorced in 1929 at age 46, settled in London, and returned to writing to support herself. During this period, she wrote women's columns, short stories, fiction reviews, and a play, *Many Women* (1932). She also collaborated on an autobiographical account of a White Russian nurse's experiences during World War I, *The Kinsmen Know How to Die* (1931).

In 1933, at age 50, she became involved with analytic psychology and trained under Carl Jung. In 1939, she published *Toward Relationship*, a Jungian exploration of masculine and feminine roles that anticipated major feminist themes. Scott-Maxwell spent World War II immersed in analytic practice in Edinburgh. After the war, she began to write again and moved her practice to Exeter. She became a commentator on the BBC on subjects such as aging, loneliness, and sex roles. In 1957, at age 74, she published a second Jungian book, *Women and Sometimes Men*.

In 1968, at age 85, Scott-Maxwell published her most successful work, the much-praised journal, *The Measure of My Days*. Scott-Maxwell died 11 years later on March 6, 1979, at age 95.

THE JOURNAL

The journal consists of 122 entries of varying length. There are numerous short entries of about 50–100 words and one long entry that runs to 6 pages. With three exceptions that occur about two thirds of the way into the book, the entries are not dated. The journal does not start on a definite date, nor does it end on a definite date. Because the book begins with the words, "We who are old . . . ," the reader is immediately placed in an unanchored expanse of time somewhere within the realm of old age. Moreover, this is very much an interior realm. With the important exceptions centering on the three dated entries, there is hardly any narration of events. The reader knows that Scott-Maxwell is in pain, but the sources of the pain are initially only hinted at. We know that she is prompted to have concerns about the fate of humanity by the events of the world, but the specific events that lead to her ruminations are not described. We also know that within her limited physical capacity she reads, but with one exception she does not specifically mention what she is reading. The absence of particular ties to the world mirrors the idea expressed in the book that those who have reached her point of age and frailty are outside of life, in the sense of being outside the flow of external events. Interior events dominate this journal: vivid descriptions of the feelings that age has brought about in her, reflections on the general state and fate of humanity, and her struggle to express the truth of her life.

In several entries, she discusses the purpose of the journal and her relationship with it. The journal was intended as a place where she could put down queries that were going around in her head when she was sewing or playing a "soothing-boring" game of patience. She began a game of asking questions and giving answers out of what she had read and forgotten and now thought her own, or out of her "recoils and hopes" (p. 7). In the journal, the answers are more explicitly stated than the questions, but among her questions are "What is the place of evil in the world?" "Why do people fear being individuals?" and "Is equality desirable?"

It is clear from many of the entries that Scott-Maxwell is living alone and spending most of her days in solitude. Consequently, she comes to view the note book as a companion, though not a very satisfactory one. This companion allows her to express sweeping opinions and complain about how wrong everyone else is, but it makes no rejoinder. Moreover, this companion is easily abandoned in favor of more responsive company. When about to take a trip for three weeks, she says she will leave her note book behind: "What need of a note book when one is out in the world?" (p.115)

The dated entries, found about two-thirds of the way into the book, contrast strikingly with those that precede. In the entry dated April 3 (no year), the reader learns that Scott-Maxwell has had a gall bladder operation. She was in the hospital for 12 days and then was transferred to a nursing home for an additional period of recuperation. The April 3 entry is made when she has finally—joyously—returned home: "I am home, I am home, I am home" (p. 89). That entry and several subsequent ones contain the only actual narrative found in the journal, the story of her operation, and the period of recovery. This story is not related in a strict linear style but does include descriptions of the surgeon's diagnosis, the process of weighing the risks of surgery, the experience of being prepared for surgery, the wooziness of awakening from the anesthetic, the healing of the wound and her interactions with the nurses. The operation was successful. The chronic pain hinted at in earlier entries was relieved. She describes that period of pain as one in which she had been a burden to herself, a problem to her doctors, and unconvincing to family and friends (p. 90). The entry is dramatic testimony of the potential for correct diagnosis and appropriate remediation to reinstill vigor in the life of an older person.

The energy released by being unburdened from pain is evidenced in an entry that follows those that deal with the operation and recuperation. This entry is also given a date (it is labeled "Good Friday"), and it concerns the idealization of women and women's identities. It is the longest entry in the journal and is occasioned by her rereading of Henry Adams' *Mont-Saint-Michel and Chartres.* Unlike the other entries, there is, therefore, a link to a specific action, albeit the limited action of reading. The operation also carries in its wake the only other dated entry, labeled Easter Day, in which she writes of being in a rare frame of mind when everything seems simple and the solution of life is the acceptance of God.

As is evident from the description of the dated entries, there is an oscillation of both energy and mood during the period covered in the journal. By her own account, Scott-Maxwell's physical stamina is low in the period preceding the operation, which covers the first two thirds of the book. At the same time, however, she struggles to express the ideas that fill her frail body about the great paradoxes of life. These entries are characterized by an absence of tranquillity; they verge on being distraught. The tone of the entries around the time of the operation is much different. With the increase in physical stamina, there is an increase in engagement with the world. As noted, this is the only part of the journal in which a story emerges that is sustained over several entries. Additionally, during this period she recounts the moment described above in which the distress she experiences about life's paradoxes abates and she sees a simple solution in the acceptance of God.

However, this is not the end of the journal. The period of improved physical stamina, what she terms her "shaky health" (p. 115), and relative emotional tranquillity is followed by a severe setback. As a result of her heightened energy and in a further realization of her desire to engage with the world, she decides to venture out on a three week trip. She returns to her apartment with a condition that is labeled by her physician as nervous exhaustion. The symptoms were severe headaches, numbness in the right arm and leg, and exhaustion. She worries that she may be going to have a stroke. "Being too well brought me to the low place I now occupy" (p. 117). This place of low energy is gradually but modestly transformed. Toward the end of the journal, Scott-Maxwell describes some recovery of energy and the regaining of a sense of tranquillity. It is clear that though not much happens during the period of the journal in the sense of objectively observable changes in life structure, a great deal does change for the better and for the worse in terms of the large swings of energy and mood.

Two themes are sustained throughout the oscillations of energy and mood: first, the passion for life hidden within Scott-Maxwell's frail body, and second, the ordeal of being an individual.

Passion and Frailty

The most striking and surprising element of the book is Scott-Maxwell's description of her passion for life, a passion that exists despite physical and social losses and which, if anything, is refined and sharpened by those losses. She begins her journal with the following:

> We who are old know that old age is more than disability. It is an intense and varied experience, almost beyond our capacity at times, but something to be carried high. (p. 5)

Elsewhere she writes:

> Age puzzles me. I thought it was a quiet time. My seventies were interesting, and fairly serene, but my eighties are passionate. I grow more intense as I age. (p. 13)

In the most moving passage on the intensity of her feeling for life, she writes:

Another secret we carry is that though drab outside—wreckage to the eye, mirrors a mortification—inside we flame with a wild life that is almost incommunicable. . . . It feels like the far side of precept and aim. It is just life, the natural intensity of life, and when old we have it for our reward and undoing. (pp. 32–33)

Scott-Maxwell's passion for life emerges paradoxically from the midst of her frailty. Her description of her frailty, or, more accurately, her relationship with her frailty, is particularly helpful in illuminating the experience of being old. She writes:

I used to draw, absorbed in the shapes of roots of trees, and seed pods, and flowers, but it strained my eyes and I gave it up. Then ten years ago I began to make rugs. . . . But my hands were too arthritic, it had to end, and now only music prevents my facing my thoughts. (p. 13)

And:

I long to laugh. I want to be enjoyed, but an hour's talk and I am exhausted. (p. 8)

And elsewhere:

We old people are short tempered because we suffer so. . . . Little things have become big; nothing in us works well, our bodies have become unreliable. We have to make an effort to do the simplest things. We urge now this, now that part of our flagging bodies, and when we have spurred them to further functioning we feel clever and carefree. (p. 35)

According to Scott-Maxwell, the twin issues faced by those who become frail are thoughts of invalidism and thoughts of death. Of the latter, she writes: "My only fear about death is that it will not come soon enough" (p. 75) and "When a new disability arrives I look about to see if death has come, and I call quietly, 'Death, is that you? Are you there?' So far the disability has answered, 'Don't be silly, it's me'" (p. 36).

She cannot treat the possibility of invalidism, of being a burden to others, of losing her capacity to take care of herself, with the humor present in the passages about death. Commenting on her feelings about having surgery, she says:

> I had one fear. What if something went wrong, and I became an invalid? What if I became a burden, ceased to be a person and became a problem, a patient, someone who could not die? (p. 91)

And later:

> I don't like to write this down, yet it is much in the minds of the old. We wonder how much older we have to become, and what degree of decay we may have to endure. (p. 138)

A key point here is that this woman's increasing frailty and concomitant reduction of activities create the conditions for an intense involvement with the essence of life, with the nonphysical aspects of humanness, with ideas themselves. She says:

> Old people are not protected from life by engagements, or pleasures, or duties; we are open to our own sentience; we cannot get away from it, and it is too much. (p. 14)

And: "To be dominated by abstract ideas is part of the helplessness of age" (p. 58).

The reduction of activities brought about by her frailty and the transition into the status of old age lead Scott-Maxwell to feel cut off from the broader social world. Near the beginning of the journal she writes:

> Being old I am out of step, troubled by my lack of concord, unable to like or understand much that I see. Feeling at variance with the times must be the essence of age. (p. 5)

Later, she writes: "We old people are not in modern life. Our impressions of it are at second or third hand. It is something we cannot know." (p. 136)

As in the case of the reduction of activities due to her frailty, the consequence for Scott-Maxwell of detachment from the social world is, paradoxically, not less involvement with life, but more. She is explicit on this point, asserting, "Now that I have withdrawn from the active world I am more alert to it than ever before" (p. 5). Also, far from not caring about the events of the world, she cares very deeply:

> Old people have so little personal life that the impact of the impersonal is sharp. Some of us feel like sounding boards, observing, reading; the outside event startles us and we ask in alarm, "Is this good or bad? To where will it lead?" (pp. 5–6)

The Ordeal of Becoming an Individual

The Vision of Individuality

Scott-Maxwell's reflections turn again and again to her vision of what it means to be fully human. This vision is based on the idea that the central human responsibility is to be an individual, to realize one's uniqueness. Her vision is wonderfully captured in a statement made near the beginning of the journal: "I am myself with ardour" (p. 19).

As an axiom of living, being an individual is easy to state but difficult to achieve. The difficulty arises, according to Scott-Maxwell, because of the comfort people get from adhering to the beliefs and prescriptions of others, rather than being true to their own way. She compares the beliefs acquired from others to a "crowd in us" and writes about the necessity of emerging from the crowd (p. 26). This is not easy to do. People dislike difference. Our acquired beliefs protect us from the danger of being an individual and therefore of being disliked for being different.

Despite the difficulty and the danger of trying to be an individual, Scott-Maxwell believes this distressing process should not be avoided. It is a sacred duty (p. 21), man's most essential task (p. 62), to live one's individual fate. The journal's strongest language is applied to descriptions of the struggle that people are bound to undergo in order to fulfill the overriding imperative of being an individual. She writes, for example, of the "ordeal of being true to your own inner way" (p. 21), of "heroic helplessness" (p. 24), of the "combat of life" (p. 27), and repeatedly of the necessity for courage. She compares the process of becoming an individual to the most painful of births: "What birth is as painful as this, a birth that may be a death, but may also be one's holy gift to one's fellows" (p. 26). The birthing of a self is a lifetime endeavor: "It has taken me all the time I've had to become myself" (p. 76). It makes her feel intoxicated and her frail physical body can barely contain what feels like an enormous presence within her, as when she was in the last months of her pregnancies and the children within claimed her body, her strength and her breath.

As powerful as her language is in describing her conviction about the importance of becoming an individual, she finds that words are inadequate to express precisely what she is trying to convey. In one entry, she regrets the absence of a word that expresses the sacred duty to be an individual. She seeks a word that signifies the "passionate conviction that one can, and should, stand by what one is, but may not seem to be" (p. 121) and rejects both self-respect and self-protection as inadequate to the task.

Giving birth to the individual that is inside does not necessarily mean that the person that emerges is wholly likable. Scott-Maxwell makes repeated reference to her incorrigible faults. She sees herself as over critical, egocentric, and vulnerable. These are defects she has known and struggled with her entire life. Having arrived at old age with the same faults she has sought to correct throughout her life, she has developed an affectionate familiarity with them: "I know my faults so well that I pay them small heed. They are stronger than I am. They are me" (p. 18).

Although the process of becoming an individual is an ordeal throughout life, aging makes it even more so. The losses associated with aging attack the sense of self built up over a lifetime. Scott-Maxwell is, in effect, asking whether it is possible to preserve one's individuality in the face of the loss of the capacity for independent action: "It takes increasing courage to be 'I' as one's frailty increases" (p. 130–131). The sheer difficulty of living, the "hardness of life" (p. 85), requires a kind of heroism, albeit an unwilling heroism, from older people: "Greatness is required of us" (p. 85).

The description she gives us of her hospitalization highlights the difficulty frail older people face in being true to themselves and maintaining a sense of integrity. Scott-Maxwell is explicit and caustic about consciously adopting the role of patient in the days of profound weakness following her operation: "I must do my work of being a patient with care. . . . Patients must like and dislike as little as possible" (p. 93). As she got stronger, her passion for being herself reawakened:

> Then the rage I knew so well rose in me and threatened all. I heard the animal growl in me when they did all the things it is my precious privacy and independence to do for myself. I hated them while I breathed, "Thank you, nurse." (p. 94)

What in Scott-Maxwell's view is the justification for engaging in the ordeal of being an individual, especially when the physical losses of aging make it so difficult? She provides two answers. First, she asserts that all those who have helped enlarge life have been strongly individual (p. 28). In her reflections on this theme, she raises the idea of evolution. She believes that the evolutionary advance of the human species is achieved through the successive activities of individuals who have stood out from the masses. Being an individual is therefore a way to advance humanity. Second, she proposes

that by truly living one's life one achieves a form of immortality (p. 40). She does not believe in personal immortality, but
she does believe that by living our own life we create something, akin to a gift, that is added to "the store from which we
came" (p. 40).

Individuality and Inequality

Many of the journal entries are devoted to exploring the
tension between the vision of individuals striving to differ-
entiate themselves from others and the ideological commitment to equality, which was being voiced so prominently
during the period when the journal was written. Scott-
Maxwell's commitment to the value of becoming an individual
leads her to value all kinds of differences. She decries the
longing not to have differences (p. 48). From her perspective,
attempts to achieve equality too often are linked to a decrease
in individuality and large scale conformity. She fears, for example, that in seeking to modernize, non-Western peoples will
imitate all aspects of Western civilization. To do so would be
a mistake. The West owes the rest of humanity a warning that
we are bad guides to follow: Follow your own way, we should
say, but don't follow us.

Similarly, she is ambivalent about women's struggle for
equality. She describes women's inferiority as a wound that
gave her aches all her life. Men stress it, she says, as though
their superiority was not safe unless women's inferiority was
proven again and again (p. 100). But despite the painful experience of being labeled inferior, she acknowledges differences between men and women which she cannot ignore. She
even asserts that men have gifts and strengths that women
lack. Moreover, in Scott-Maxwell's view, women are guilty of
some of what men hold against them: "[W]omen are the meeting place of the highest and lowest" (p. 105). She reaches a
point of resolution on this issue that is consistent with her
commitment to valuing differences:

Perhaps we must say to man "You create us when you love us, but you destroy us both when you stress our inferiority. The time may have come for us to forge our own identity, dangerous as that will be." (p. 105)

In keeping with her valuing of differences between persons, Scott-Maxwell values differentiation in the sense of discrimination and evaluation. She rails against the modern will to be undifferentiated (p. 49) and the demand to be accepted without assessment. She sees the failure to judge as a relinquishment of the responsibility of the individual (p. 50).

She is aware that her defense of inequality could be construed as a kind of heartlessness or dishonoring of someone who had less than she. Nonetheless, she persists in her defense of inequality, claiming that inequality is inherent in nature and that to deny it is to lose oneself in pretense.

The wish for equality, the drift toward relativism, and the denial of the possibility of superiority undercut the sense of accomplishment. Inequality, in the sense of the recognition that others may be our superiors, may lead to resentment, envy and hate. Yet, to deny inequality is to close off the possibility of admiration, improvement and progress:

Must all the gifts of those greater than we disappear from the world? No triumphs of accomplishment? No drive to discover the rare in ourselves and others? Never to be bemused by beauties we lack? No sudden insight of what might be? No respect or loyalty or humility stirred by what you had not known was possible? But these are our ennobling moments. It is at these times we outgrow ourselves. (p. 59)

In elaborating a vision of the sacred duty to be individual, Scott-Maxwell's journal traces the link between the personal and the political. We are duty bound to develop what is in us. This necessarily produces differences among people in society, not only of kind but also of degree (i.e., some people are better than others with regard to certain attributes). Choosing to gloss over such differences on the basis of a devotion to equality and a concomitant relativistic orientation to making judgments sacrifices the potential for human expansion. The task, therefore, is to respect difference and try to understand it.

COMMENTARY

Individuation

Individuation in Jung

The idea of the struggle to become an individual, articulated so prominently in Scott-Maxwell's journal, is a major feature of the thinking of her mentor, C. G. Jung. Jung uses the term individuation to designate this process (Goldbrunner, 1964; Jung, 1933; Moore & Fine, 1990).

According to Jung, individuation begins with the recognition that people, particularly in the first half of life, develop an automatic way of responding to the surrounding world. It is as if a kind of mask develops that hides the individual's true nature. Jung calls this outer covering the *Persona*, from the Latin word for the mask worn by actors in classical times. The Persona is the system of relationships between the consciousness of the individual and society. The concept of Persona shares conceptual territory with the sociological concept of role and G. H. Mead's concept of the *me*.

Although the Persona is not inherently pathological, people can identify themselves too closely with their Personas. They come to imagine that they are what they represent. Examples include the official who has become identical with the part he plays, the salesman who is constantly engaged in selling, and the always friendly, polite lady whose behavior is never flawed. According to the theory, anyone who overidentifies with the Persona will be subject to moods, fears, hallucinations, and weaknesses concealed from the eyes of others, but evident in private life. The process is like that of symptom formation related to repression described by Freud. In this case the repression is of the personal and collective unconscious.

The goal of the process of individuation is to achieve an objective attitude toward one's personality, to achieve harmony between the inner and outer life, and to be to the outside world what one is from within. Individuation involves parting from the Persona, detaching oneself from it as clearly as possible. For Jung, this process does not really begin until after age 40, the meridian of life. Separation from the Persona opens the individual to the contents of the personal unconscious. Everything that had been repressed becomes alive. People come to acknowledge the shadow side of their personalities, the morally disreputable and unpleasant aspects of the heretofore spotless ego.

The process of differentiating from the Persona and the assimilation of the personal unconscious make one sensitive in a new way to the outside world. With individuation comes an increasing ability to perceive and respond to objects in the world (notably other persons) as they really are, rather than on the basis of projections that turn them into illusory objects derived from unconscious desires. Thus, individuation can be said to involve separation, the formation of clearer boundaries between the person and the world.

The process of individuation also leads to contact with the collective unconscious within each of us. The collective unconscious is manifested in the archetypes that inhabit the human psyche. Especially significant among these archetypes are the anima, the female shadow in men, and the animus, the male shadow in women. Individuation involves objectivizing the archetypes, coming to appreciate their presence within the mind and learning to discern when our actions unconsciously emanate from them.

The ego is permanently altered through objectivization of the archetypes. The ego comes to take the unconscious into account. The feeling is one of a new and slowly developing center of personality. The center is no longer the ego (consciousness), but rather a point between consciousness and the unconscious. Jung terms this point the self. Individuation is, in effect, the development or creation of self, understood in this way. Persons are described as centered when the shift from the ego to the self has occurred. Jung likens this process to a Copernican revolution: "It is as though the ego were the earth, and it suddenly discovered that the sun (or the self) was the centre of the planetary orbits and of the earth's orbit as well" (Jung, 1933, p. 70).

In this view, the process of personality formation extends to the end of life. Life itself is like a forge; the self is molded by life. Only death brings this process to an end. Thus, Jung's theory is consonant with contemporary perspectives that emphasize developmental potentials throughout the life course.

Individuation in Levinson

Jung's concept of individuation plays a central role in Levinson's model of the life cycle (see Chapter 3). As Levinson uses the concept, individuation means becoming more uniquely individual through a changed relationship with the world. In successive periods of development, as the process of individuation goes on the person forms a clearer boundary between self and world.

Levinson conceives of the process of individuation, of redefining the boundary between self and world, as occurring throughout the life course, but he views it as especially salient in transition periods such as infancy, adolescence, and mid-life. In infancy, the newborn must gain some idea of its separate existence and must learn where self stops and world begins. Starting at about five months, there is a psychological birth of the infant as an individuated center of consciousness (Mahler et al., 1975). In adolescence, ties of dependency to the preadult world must be loosened and the process of forming an adult identity initiated. These earlier key developmental moments in the process of individuation form the background to Levinson's main concern, mid-life individuation. Individuation at mid-life involves modification of the early adult self and development of a new life structure more appropriate for middle adulthood.

For Levinson, the process of individuation can be analyzed in terms of four polarities. The polarities should be understood as irreconcilable tensions at the ground of human existence. The anchoring poles of the pairs are not mutually exclusive but, rather, exist simultaneously in each person. The four polarities are young–old, destruction–creation, attachment–separateness, and masculine–feminine. The young-old polarity pertains to people's sense of themselves as young or old, how old a person feels. This feeling is independent of chronological age: Young people can feel old and old people can feel young. One of Levinson's major points is that mid-life marks the passage from membership in the younger generation of society to membership in the senior generation. There are many reminders that one is no longer young. The tension comes about because of the continuing fluctuation in the way we feel about ourselves on this dimension.

The destruction–creation polarity relates to the way that destruction and creation are intertwined. Efforts to create or to do good in the world are achieved at a cost. The decision to hire one applicant for a job harms the applicant who is not selected. A divorce may benefit one or both partners but destroys the marriage.

The attachment–separateness polarity refers to the tension between striving to be with and do for others versus being with and doing for oneself. Discussion of this tension was presented in Chapter 4 in connection with the journals of May Sarton. The masculine–feminine polarity pertains to the fundamental bisexuality of humans, the idea that we are all both masculine and feminine and must reach an accommodation with both of these facets of ourselves.

The polarities exist during the entire life cycle and can never be fully resolved or transcended. Individuation consists of confronting them and reaching a revised response to the polarities. With each successive wave of responses to the polarities, the past life structure is given up to a greater or lesser degree and a new life structure is initiated.

Individuation in Scott-Maxwell

Scott-Maxwell's vision of the individual is suffused with elements of her teacher Jung's concept of individuation and is consonant with the elaboration of the concept of individuation developed by Levinson. When she writes of the comfort people get from adhering to the beliefs acquired from others and the way that beliefs protect us from the danger of being an individual, she is essentially describing what Jung would call the challenge of differentiating oneself from one's Persona, with her description coming "from the inside," from one who has experienced the pain of separation from the Persona. Similarly, in voicing her recognition of and relationship with her faults ("I know my faults. . . . They are me") she is alluding to what, from a Jungian perspective, might be termed the abandonment of the spotless ego and her acceptance of the disreputable aspects of the total person she is. Scott-Maxwell is explicit about the experience that was central to her individuation and her evolution as a person. Consistent with the Jungian theory, she views her personal discovery of the unconscious within her as the pivotal event of her life: "The most important thing in my life was the rich experience of the unconscious. This was a gift life gave me and I only had the sense to honour and serve it" (pp. 75–76). Finally, in keeping with Jung's idea that individuation is a lifelong process, as described above, Scott-Maxwell gives voice to the experience of the hard work of continuing the process of individuation in the face of increasing frailty.

Aspects of individuation highlighted by Levinson are also evident in Scott-Maxwell's journal. Her vision of the individual struggling to separate from the crowd echoes Levinson's discussion of individuation as a process in which new boundaries are created between self and world. Additionally, as with Levinson's polarities, Scott-Maxwell gives great emphasis to the inevitability of conflict and the tension of opposites. At various points in the journal, she addresses each of Levinson's four polarities. Moreover, there are repeated descriptions of life being a process that entails successive encounters with irreconcilable oppositions which are always only partially resolved: "We crave for that which lies behind the terrible play of the opposites. We pray to have the conflict resolved, but life would end if it were resolved" (p. 84).

Scott-Maxwell and Transference Heroics

The ordeal of individuation as presented in Scott-Maxwell's journal has strong resonances with Becker's concept of transference heroics that was discussed in Chapter 6. With Becker, Scott-Maxwell recognizes that many people achieve their heroism by conforming to societal prescriptions for right behavior. They both recognize that beliefs acquired from others provide a protective shield that is difficult to escape. Like Becker, Scott-Maxwell conceives of the tension of opposites as being fundamental to human existence. Although she does not elaborate the dialectic between fear of life and the fear of death in the way that Becker does, Scott-Maxwell does view the twin motives of attachment and separateness as powerful human tendencies. As she puts it,

> Differing and belonging . . . [are] so important that without those two strong threads binding each other there would be no living cloth, usable and durable. How much containment is necessary, of how much daring and originality are we capable? (p. 70)

Scott-Maxwell understands, along with Becker, that there is a certain arbitrariness to what we construe to be the imperatives of our lives at a given developmental moment. What Jung terms individuation, Becker would term *transference heroics*, that is, striving to construct a beyond which more fully draws out the self. The process of individuation casts new light on old forms of heroics:

> What felt at moments like the white heat of necessity was much my own doing, and it may have been a wrong–headed effort. I shall never know. (pp. 29–30)

What Scott-Maxwell fails to see, however, is that, as pointed out by Becker, even the most individualistic of people have their transference objects. They identify with and subject themselves to a reality beyond the self.

Aging and Personal Liberation

To what extent is the process of becoming more individuated described by Scott-Maxwell typical of older people? Alternatively, does aging create the potential for individuation, a potential that is realized in some but not other older people? Clearly, neither of these questions can be answered based on this single personal journal. Scott-Maxwell, herself, is aware of her tendency to generalize from her own experience to that of all older people. Out of her firm conviction of the value of difference, she recoils at her own tendency to speak for the aged: "I write my notes as though I spoke for all old people. This is nonsense" (p. 120). Elsewhere she comments that old people can seldom say "we"; they are alone with the experience of age (p. 130).

Yet, there are hints from other researchers and observers of the aged that Scott-Maxwell is speaking not just of her own experience but of a more general phenomenon. Aging may lead to increasing individuality, decreasing conformity, and a loosening of commitment to conventionality. The idea that release from conformity and increasing personal liberation are developmental potentials of later life has been discussed by Kuypers (1977), Moody (1988), and Tobin (1991).

Basing his observations, in part, on his pioneering 40-year longitudinal study (Maas & Kuypers, 1974), Kuypers (1977) proposes that aging creates the potential for personal liberation. His discussion focuses on the way that transitions often represent a release from prior obligations and a rebirth of new interests and personal freedoms. He considers an important life task of old age to be the development of a sense of confidence and trust in one's ability to act in self-directed ways with the conviction that the ultimate test of value resides within. He also notes that the relative social invisibility of older people may allow greater personal freedom. Older people are released from the human-worth-equals-social-utility equation. They also are relatively free from the constant obligation to make choices that characterizes middle adulthood, a point also mentioned by Scott-Maxwell. Kuypers concludes that older people are in a better position to know themselves clearly and to use that knowledge to make choices that count.

While criticizing stage theories such as Erikson's stages of psychosocial development or Kohlberg's stages of moral development as containing a covert ideology in which the highest stage of consciousness turns out to coincide with the last stage of life, Moody (1988) comments that many old people experience their lives much as Scott-Maxwell described her life, as an awakening from domination. This is highly significant for Moody, who argues for reconstituting gerontology as an emancipatory discourse. The primary goal of such a discourse is empowerment in the practice of freedom. For Moody, late life is potentially a period of freedom and fulfillment and can become an opening through which the dominating forces of the state and the marketplace can be seen for what they are (p. 35). From the perspective Moody is advocating, the

Scott-Maxwell journal is a key text which articulates a central theme in older persons' experiences of the life world.

The awakening from domination that is potentiated in later life may include release from lifelong internal conflicts. In discussing the unique psychology of the very old, Tobin (1991) describes the way that the old can allow into consciousness feelings and motives they previously disowned. Destructive and envious urges can be acknowledged without the anxiety and self-reproach that would have occurred had such feelings reached awareness earlier in life. Tobin views this release from conflict as leading to increase in self-understanding. He considers such an increase in self-understanding as linked to what he proposes as the central task of later life, preserving the self. Previously unwelcome aspects of self are useful for self-definition. As noted above, Scott-Maxwell puts it this way: "I know my faults. . . . They are me."

In keeping with Kuypers', Moody's and Tobin's observations, Scott-Maxwell's journal can, then, be read as a powerful statement of the potential for individuation and personal liberation in the face of frailty.

The idea of the self, which plays such a key role in Scott-Maxwell's journal, is never far from the center stage in the other journals we have considered. Indeed, reflection on the self was one of the criteria for identifying a work as a personal journal of later life. It is time to give fuller consideration to the elusive topic of the self.

Diaries, Narrative, and the Self

8

The term personal journals was introduced in Chapter 2 to establish a common feature among the diaries discussed in this book. The common feature is that the day-to-day experience of the writer is taken as the primary subject of the work. This is in contrast to diaries whose principal aim is to recount events without regard to the way those events are experienced.

When writers take their experience as the continuing subject of diary entries, we might innocently say "they are writing about themselves." However, that innocent expression has embedded within it an idea that is far from simple: the idea of the self.

The "self" constitutes a central concept and continuing problem in philosophy and psychology. One psychologist whose work on the self is an exemplary synthesis of empirical psychology and philosophy has termed the self a mirage, a concept deemed to be at the center of human experience and yet impossible to grasp (Ryff, 1989).

The goal of this chapter is to select from the plethora of approaches to the self in philosophy and psychology the ideas that are most germane to the study of journals of later life.

165

We will start with a fundamental distinction in discussions about the self between the self-as-knower and self-as-known. This will be followed by an elaboration on the idea of the self-as-known. The final sections of the chapter present the idea of the shifting horizon of self-understanding and an illustration of that idea in the journals of May Sarton.

THE KNOWER AND THE KNOWN

A basic observation about the concept of self is the distinction between the self-as-knower (or self-as-subject) and the self-as-known (or self-as-object). As soon as we turn our attention toward ourselves, we become aware of needing to distinguish between the imagined object of our thought, the self as we conceive it, and the self that is doing the conceiving. The touchstone for discussions of this distinction is the following statement from William James:

> Whatever I may be thinking of, I am always at the same time more or less aware of *myself*, of my *personal existence*. At the same time it is *I* who am aware; so that the total self of me, being as it were duplex, partly known and partly knower, partly object and partly subject, must have two aspects discriminated in it, of which for shortness we may call one the *Me* and the other the *I*. (James, 1961, p. 41, emphasis in original)

This distinction also formed the basis of the influential work of George Herbert Mead. Mead saw the I as the subject of all action, the spontaneous aspect of the self. The Me, in contrast, was the repository of all past actions.

In terms of the personal journal, the distinction between the I and the Me aspects of the self is particularly salient. The personal journal is a written record of the self-as-known, an objectification created by the self-as-knower.

Contemporary theorizing about the self continues to employ this distinction. For example, a comprehensive review of aging and self-conceptions begins by harking back to James's distinction between the I and the Me in order to establish an organizing perspective for the vast literature in gerontology using the idea of self (Bengtson, Reddy, & Gordon, 1985). Interestingly, this review then goes on to identify its focus as exclusively on the self-as-known. That is, the authors quite correctly acknowledge that research on self-conceptions is, by definition, research on the self-as-known.

The distinction between the I and the Me was also usefully employed in a review of the child development literature on the self (Harter, 1983). There, also, it was noted that research on the self-as-known has dominated. The self-as knower, as process, as active agent, has received far less attention. But whereas in the past research focused almost exclusively on the self-as-known, the cognitive revolution in psychology has led to new emphasis on the self-as-knower. The self-as-knower has been characterized as a predominantly tacit, process-based and fully embodied working theory of itself and the world (Mahoney, 1991, p. 224). The term *theory* in this context does not imply an explicitly articulated set of beliefs, but rather an abstract and open set of organizing principles. In this view, when we speak of the self-as-knower, we are really speaking of the organizing processes that *are* each person in his or her moment-to-moment becoming. James's I, then, becomes, in contemporary parlance, the self-as-information processor.

The distinction between the I and the Me is helpful for analytic purposes, but can also be deceptive. The I and the Me are not distinct entities. The I aspect of self and the Me aspect exist in relationship to each other; that relationship is dialectical (Sherman, 1991).

The I–Me dialectic refers to the ongoing activity of characterizing ourselves to ourselves and to others. The I side of the dialectic is a person's "core ordering processes" (Mahoney, 1991). The Me side of the dialectic is objectification of self in language. Objectification here includes all kinds of self-statements, ranging from casual remarks to friends about the "way we are," to responses to structured questionnaires and entries in journals. Each such characterization amounts to an attempt to cast experience into language. In psychology, we used to speak of this activity of formulating self-statements as "self-perception," as if the self were simply and passively read off of some sort of virtual computer screen. The term *perception* in the phrase *self-perception* masked the constructed nature of self-as-known. The self, in the sense of the self-as-known, is not perceived—it is *conceived*. In the contemporary view, we recognize that each characterization of the self is an interpretive effort, like the process used by an historian or an anthropologist trying to understand a period or a people (Bruner, 1990).

The dialectical nature of the relationship between I and Me is seen in the way that characterizations people offer of themselves influence their subsequent self-characterizations. To continue the metaphor of the person as historian or anthropologist of himself or herself, it is as if once an official history has been proclaimed in a culture and enters the public domain, that very fact alters the process of constructing subsequent histories. For the most part, the influence is that of a kind of crystallization. The constructed version of the self resists change. There is a great deal of force on the side of continuity in terms of the core features of one's representations of self, others and relationships (Gergen & Gergen, 1988; Mahoney, 1991). Sometimes, however, the objectified version of the self, what is revealed as a result of the interpretive activity, can change. After hearing what they have said about themselves—or, in the case of personal journals, reading it— people are sometimes prompted to take action to prove themselves wrong. As noted in Chapter 5, proving herself wrong was a regular pastime of Doris Grumbach. We can identify other situations in which people have provided accounts of their lives or some aspect of their lives (versions of the Me), which they perceived to be accurate or at least plausible, but which they come to devalue or reject.

A particularly compelling recent example is found in a chapter by Jacquelyn Wiersma (1992). Wiersma summarizes a series of life stories told by Karen, who was interviewed as part of a longitudinal study of women who had changed from a domestic career (as wife and mother) to one outside the home.

At age 31, Karen, married to a university faculty member and with an 18-month-old child, returned to college. At that time she viewed this activity not as the shedding of her domestic career, but rather as a way to become a responsible faculty wife. She stated, "I was very clear I should be primarily oriented toward my husband. I worried about what people thought about me and whether I was dressed right and whether I was playing the role of faculty wife right" (p. 197). To be a good wife, she would have to become intellectually adept. In college, she decided to study history, with an emphasis on the influence of children on the family.

She went on to graduate school and while still a graduate student, rose to national prominence through an organization promoting grass-roots historical societies. All the while, however, she continued overtly to subscribe to the wifely role. At the point of her initial interview with Wiersma, she felt stuck in her graduate student role and was unable to complete her dissertation and move ahead toward faculty member status.

Interestingly, the very act of telling her story to Wiersma seemed to consolidate for Karen a mounting ambivalence about the Me of her story. In rereading the transcript of her initial interview, she began to look at herself apart from the role of wife and mother. She had perceived herself as unfree (see discussion of transference heroics in Chapter 6), but she began, consciously and publicly, to think in terms of freedom. In later interviews, she described thinking about challenging herself in productive ways outside the norms of the wife–

mother role. She began to question the priority she had made
of her husband's wishes and to confront him about his family responsibilities. She came to perceive the roots of her
uncritical acceptance of the wife–mother role as a reenact-
ment of certain elements of her parents' marriage. The questioning, the dawning realizations, and the sense of escape from
old constraints led to a burst of energy that enabled her to
complete her dissertation.

It is certainly possible that Karen would have changed without the experience of serving as a subject in a study that required her to objectify her sense of herself by articulating her
life story. Nonetheless, Wiersma's account makes it clear that
the feedback that Karen got from *listening to her own story*
served as a powerful spur to action.

A similar process seems to have taken place for May Sarton.
In *Plant Dreaming Deep*, Sarton created an image of herself
as a "wise old party." She provided a stirring, romantic por-
trait of a woman who faced and overcame adversity and who
had developed a solid sense of self based on her ties to community and history. The only problem was that the story was
too pat. As Sarton wrote in *Journal of a Solitude*, she did not
at all resemble the wise old party of *Plant Dreaming Deep*. To
the contrary she was more typically on an emotional roller
coaster, "up to heaven and down to hell in an hour" (p. 12).

FURTHER REFLECTIONS ON THE SELF-AS-KNOWN

Suppose, as has been done thousands of times in introductory psychology classes, we give someone a piece of paper and
at the top write in the words "Who am I?" and underneath
place 10 lines and ask for 10 answers to that question on the
lines that have been provided. What happens?

It is important to recognize that the responses to the question "Who am I?" constitute objectifications of the self. To
respond to the question posed in the introductory psychol-

ogy class, the I characterizes itself and, in so doing, creates a Me. If the subjects cooperate, the typical responses are traits (e. g., "honest," "confused," "friendly") and roles (e. g., "son," "student," "American"). From this, we might infer that the Me or identity consists of a bundle of such discrete characterizations.

Although people can and often do characterize themselves and others in terms of traits and roles, if we allow people the freedom to characterize themselves in a format that does not restrict them to a series of discrete words or phrases, we are likely to get something quite different from the responses to the "Who am I?" quiz. As Gergen and Gergen (1988) have noted, in our experience of ourselves and others we seem to encounter not a series of discrete endlessly juxtaposed moments, but of goal-directed sequences. To understand is to place events within a context of preceding and subsequent events. One's view of oneself in a given moment is fundamentally nonsensical unless it can be linked in some fashion with one's own past. When asked to describe themselves and allowed freedom of response, people seem to naturally begin to tell stories (Mishler, 1986). Although people are perfectly capable of offering a summary judgment about themselves as being, for instance, poetic, it makes no sense to view such a statement as emerging without some rootedness in time. Rather, such a self-characterization would have embedded in it a narrative of past actions, which would warrant application of the descriptor. Narratives, stories of the self, lie at the core of people's conceptions of themselves.

Our understanding of the relationship between responses to the "Who am I?" questionnaire and the storied nature of identity can be advanced by turning to Paul Ricoeur's (1992) discussion of personal identity. Ricoeur points out that in describing people and reidentifying them from one occasion to the next, we do rely on the language of dispositions. What is often overlooked, however, is that such dispositions are acquired, that is, they have histories. Ricoeur considers two types of dispositions: habits and identifications. Personal identity is, in part, constituted of habits. Habits can be thought of as behavioral responses to the environment. Ricoeur points out that everything that is habit was, at one time, a new response, which over time became a habitutated response. His point about habits is similar to that made by Dannefer and Perlmutter (1990), who conceive of habit—what they term *environmental habitutation*, as one of three fundamental processes of developmental change, along with physical ontogeny and cognitive generativity.

A second form of disposition considered by Ricoeur is the identification. To a large extent, the self-as-known is made up of identifications with values, norms, ideals, models, heroes (McAdams, 1988). However, such identifications are also acquired and to say that identifications are acquired is to say they have histories.

Because of the acquired nature of habits and identifications it is possible, in principle at least, to trace back their origin and reconstruct how any given habit or identification was acquired. Such a reconstruction would be in the form of a narrative account.

Ricoeur (1992) uses the phenomenological term *sedimentation* to label the process by which temporally-rooted narratives are abstracted into dispositions. Sedimentation involves, in effect, a contraction of experience. However, "what sedimentation has contracted, narration can redeploy" (p. 122). It is possible to expand the sedimented dispositions we use to label ourselves back within the movement of narration. Each disposition can, as it were, be unpacked.

To return to the "Who am I?" questionnaire, the responses take the form of discrete, timeless dispositions. However, each disposition has its own story, which, with patience, could be recovered. Does that mean that the Me, instead of being a set of discrete traits, is a set of discrete narratives?

It is difficult to imagine unpacking a set of responses to the "Who am I?" questionnaire without quickly getting involved in the relationships among the narratives out of which the traits emerged. That is, I may describe myself as both determined and uncertain, but it is not unlikely that the accounts I would provide for labeling myself in these terms would be intertwined. I could tell you the story of how I am determined to achieve a particular goal. But that story could very well be intertwined with the story of my uncertainty about what goals I should set or of my failure to achieve goals in the past. In fact, the unpacking and intertwining of responses to a modified version of the "Who am I?" questionnaire has been employed clinically (Mahoney, 1991). The narratives provided to explain a set of responses to a "Who am I?" questionnaire would readily move me in the direction of a much larger narrative, the narrative of my life. In sum, the narratives pertaining to particular traits and roles are nested in the larger narrative of the whole life.

There has been an extraordinary explosion of interest during the past decade in collecting, analyzing, and theorizing about narratives of the life course. Central to this research is the idea that such narratives foster a sense of well-being through their integration of the presently-understood past, the experienced present, and the anticipated future (Cohler, 1982). As McAdams has put it, such narratives are "the stories we live by" (McAdams, 1993). The self-story serves to *emplot* life events with meanings.

Self-stories are text-like entities resembling literary productions. They are, in effect, works of fiction (Denzin, 1989a). Self-narratives are not created *ex nihilo*. Rather, they draw on templates provided by other stories in a culture. Narratives adapt experience to the social context of meaning (Murray, 1989). They are necessarily conventionalized expressions of experience, social constructions. They are historically-effected (Gadamer, 1960/1992), that is, brought about by virtue of our existence in an historically emerging culture.

Because of the literary-like quality of life stories, investigators have turned to literary criticism to analyze and classify these texts of identity. For example, several researchers have used Northrop Frye's (1957) delineation of four fundamental story forms—tragedy, romance, comedy and irony—to categorize life stories (Gergen & Gergen, 1988; Murray, 1989; Schafer, 1976). Others (Bruner, 1990; Sherman, 1991) have used Amelie Rorty's (1976) characterization of the protagonists in Western folk tales and fiction into figures, persons, and individuals, as a basis for analyzing the form of agency assumed by the narrator in telling the story of his or her life.

A third critical framework for categorizing stories, which has great potential value for the analysis of self-stories, is that proposed by Sacks (1967). Sacks uses the term *action* to designate a type of prose fiction in which characters about whose fates we care are introduced into unstable relationships that are then further complicated until the complication is finally resolved by the complete removal of the instability. He identifies three forms of actions. Comic actions are those in which the reader's expectation from the outset is that, despite complications, the "good guys" and the "bad guys" will receive their ethical deserts. Tragic actions are those in which the expectation is that the characters with whose fates we are most concerned are doomed and make choice after choice which leads to inevitable misery. Serious actions are those in which the final stabilization of relationships is unclear. The story may end happily or unhappily for the characters with whom we are most in sympathy. In a phrase particularly relevant to the study of lives, Sacks refers to the these three forms as *narrative powers* realized by actions. Applying these terms to self-stories, we could think of those which realize a comic power, in which the narrator triumphs over adversity and everything comes out all right; stories that realize a tragic power, in which it is clear that the narrator has failed and will continue to fail; and self-stories that realize a serious power, in which it is not clear what the outcome will be.

In addition to these typologies of narratives, as noted in Chapter 2, it is a characteristic of the life course in contemporary Western societies that there appears to be a single master template which emerged in the Renaissance and continues to the present: the idea of the centrality and sovereignty of the individual (Sampson, 1985; Shotter & Gergen, 1989; Weintraub, 1978).

The self-story is not a fixed entity. It first emerges in recognizable form in late adolescence (McAdams, 1988). At that age people begin the activity of self-biography that continues for the rest of life. The process begins with the development of a set of repudiations and assimilations of childhood identifications into a configuration that includes plot, character, settings, scenes, and themes. The initial story is continually reworked. As is the case with interpreting any literary text, all self-interpretations are unfinished and inconclusive. The self-story is constantly being created as it is lived; the meanings of the pieces change as new patterns are found. Sometimes, there is a substantial realignment of the elements of the self-story—a new set of interpretations of past events and current experiences. Such radical revisions of self-stories underlie what we recognize as identity transformation in adulthood.

Although maintaining a coherent life story is a developmental task from adolescence onward, aging poses difficult challenges to people's ability to maintain narrative coherence (Cohler & Galatzer-Levy, 1990). The challenges arise from the inevitable losses of attachments to other persons through deaths of family and friends, losses of attachments to place through changes in communities, losses of physical and cognitive abilities, and the increasing recognition of the finitude of life.

Personal Journals and Self Stories

What is the place of personal journals against the backdrop of the narrative nature of the self-as-known?

First, like the genre of formal autobiography discussed in Chapter 2, the self-stories elicited by researchers like Kaufman, Kotre, Bruner, Sherman, and McAdams review the whole of life from a particular moment. The personal journals discussed in the preceding chapters certainly contain narratives, but they are not narratives of the whole life. Rather, they contain examples of narratives nested within the life.

Second, although personal journals do not present a single, coherent life story, based on information provided in personal journals it is often possible to infer major components of the life story that might have been elicited by an interviewer during the period in which the diary was written. As indicated in the discussions of Vining, Sarton, Grumbach, Olmstead, and Scott-Maxwell, life themes emerge in the journals much as they would in life history interviews. As Gadamer (1960/1992) notes, "Like the coherence of a text, the structural coherence of life is defined as a relation between the whole and the parts. Every part expresses something of the whole of life—i.e., has significance for the whole—just as its own significance is determined by the whole" (p. 223).

Finally, in contrast to formal autobiography diaries expose *the shifting horizon of self-understanding*. From a moving vantage point, the journal writer constantly mediates between, on the one hand, the preexisting interpretation of his or her life's meaning and direction and, on the other hand, fresh experience, which may strain that interpretation (Fothergill, 1974). The idea of the shifting horizon of self-understanding, which is so central to the nature of diaries, needs to be explored in some detail.

THE SHIFTING HORIZON
OF SELF-UNDERSTANDING

To grasp more fully the nature of self-understanding evidenced in personal journals it is necessary to return to language and concerns of hermeneutics introduced in Chapter 1 and especially to the work of Gadamer and Ricoeur.

Gadamer (1960/1992) presents an interconnected cluster of ideas pertaining to the nature of interpretation of texts. This conceptual nexus provides a rich language for describing people's interpretations of the text-like entities considered in the previous section, self-stories or life history narratives.

We have to begin by reminding ourselves that every statement about the self, that is, about the Me, is an act of interpretation. At the beginning of this chapter, the act of creating statements about the self was compared to the work of historians or anthropologists in interpreting an historical era or a culture. The Me, whether in the form of disposition statements or a full-blown self story, is not passively perceived or registered, but rather is created. And what is created is an interpretation.

A key insight provided by Gadamer is to emphasize repeatedly that any interpretive act is a historically situated event. Understanding does not transcend time; it is *in* time. The understanding we have of, for example, a novel or a work of art, is necessarily the understanding we have of it now, based on our current armamentarium of ideas and the way we have articulated out experience to ourselves to date. Such ideas and articulations can be termed *expressions of life* (Palmer, 1969, p. 112). Gadamer uses the terms *forestructures of understanding* and *traditions of interpretation* to highlight the way such expressions of life influence the moment of interpretation. In effect, any interpretation amounts to an application of our current forestructures of understanding to a text. "This is what this text means" is really shorthand for the more accurate expression "This is what this text means to me now" based on my tradition of interpretation.

When people think back over their lives, it is as if the incidents of the past exist as a sort of text, which can be woven into a coherent account. But the account that is provided, as for example in life history interviews, is always and inescapably situated in the present. The descriptions people offer about the kind of people they are or about the meaning of an incident in their day-to-day life does not hold for all time. Each objectification is an *event* of interpretation, not a timeless truth, but an act, a casting of lived experience into words.

Gadamer (1960/1992) introduces the idea of horizon, borrowed from Nietzsche and Husserl, to capture the idea that situated understanding is necessarily understanding from a standpoint—a standpoint that limits the possibility of vision. The horizon is the range of vision that includes everything that can be seen from a particular vantage point. The horizon is not a rigid boundary, but rather something into which we move and that moves with us. Meaning always stands on a horizonal context that stretches into the past and into the future (Palmer, 1969). Moreover, the passage of time means that one's horizon is always changing: "The horizon of the past, out of which all human life lives and which exists in the form of tradition, is always in motion" (Gadamer, 1960/1992, p. 304).

Personal journals exemplify this central feature of the human condition: the shifting horizon of self-understanding. The entries are events of interpretation in which the writer attempts give meaning to day-to-day incidents. In carrying out such meaning-making, the diarist draws on forestructures of understanding, the traditions for interpretation he or she has established. In this sense, every incident recorded in a diary expresses something of the whole life narrative. However, interpreted incidents also shape and constitute the *tradition*, the life narrative itself. This reciprocal relationship between the incidents recorded in journal entries and the life story as a whole, is, of course, an example of the hermeneutic circle, described in Chapter 1. Like the coherence of a text, the coherence of a life is defined as the relation between the whole and its parts. Every part expresses something of the whole life, that is, has significance for the whole, just as its significance is determined by the whole.

The passage of time shifts the horizon of self-understanding. What we see of life at age 20 is vastly different from what we see at age 40 and what we see at age 40 is vastly different from what we see at age 60 or 80. But does the shifting *horizon* of self-understanding result in a shift in the self-story? This question becomes particularly salient when we consider people's situations in their later years when they are likely to experience changes in their bodies and changes in their place in the world.

The self-story is a type of narrative and shares the characteristics of other forms of narrative compositions. Ricoeur (1992) has pointed out that in all forms of narrative there are concordant and discordant events, roughly corresponding to the expected and the unexpected. The creation of narrative, what Ricoeur terms *narrative configuration*, involves reconciling the competition between the demands for concordance and the admission of discordance, a synthesis of the heterogeneous. Narrative plots have an instability that arises through movement between concordant and discordant events. Through the dialectical process of narrative configuration, unexpected events become transfigured into narratively necessary events—chance becomes fate.

When people are asked to tell the stories of their lives, as, for example, has been done in Bruner's (1987) and Sherman's (1991) research, they select events from the past and *emplot* them into narratives (Ricoeur, 1992). The emplotment of life stories involves the reconciliation of concordant and discordant events so that the life as a whole constitutes a story. Identity becomes the self-story. The Me becomes the temporal totality of the events of our lives.

Any given narrative configuration that a person provides of his or her own life is threatened by unforseeable (discordant) events that punctuate it, such as accidents, illnesses, encounters with other people, winning the lottery, or large scale historical events such as war or depression. A discordant event may so alter our lives that what was formerly central to the life story becomes peripheral and what was formerly peripheral takes on central importance. A discordant event may thus force a reconfiguration of the life story, change a tragic self-narrative into a romantic one, or vice versa.

When people tell the story of their lives or, as in the journals, recount incidents (nested narratives) that relate to their larger life-story, the account has to be given from the present horizon of self-understanding. We make sense of the present in terms of our working theory of the kind of story we are in the middle of, the narrative power (Sacks, 1967) being realized by our life. But we do not really know what that power is and will not know until the end.

And what about the end? In the case of an older person it may be necessary for the narrator to ask "Is my story still happening or have I arrived at the end?" As the horizon of self-understanding shifts, it may become apparent that we were not in the middle of the story we thought we were in the middle of. Perhaps we thought our life was a tragedy and all along, unbeknownst to us, it was a romance. Or perhaps we thought our life was almost over, at least in terms of the future holding anything new, and it turned out there was a lot more to it.

The tracking both of the quandary of trying to ascertain what kind of narrative is being realized by one's life and of the shifting of the self-story in view of discordant events are the great strengths of the diary form. Among the journal writers considered in the book—and, perhaps, among all those who have published in the journal form—none has revealed this aspect of human functioning more than May Sarton. This chapter concludes with a consideration of the way that Sarton's sense of the meaning of her life shifted during the 20 years covered by her journals.

The Shifting Horizon of Self-Understanding in Sarton's Journals

In Chapter 4, we considered Sarton's journals in terms of the theme of the tension between attachment and separateness repeatedly found in them. Now we consider these journals from another perspective: Sarton's efforts to express her understanding of her life from within the horizon of the present, a horizon that shifts with the passage of time. The powerful impact of Sarton's journals arises, in part, through the way they expose the shifting horizon of her self-understanding. As we read the journals, we repeatedly witness her attempts to sum up the story of her life: to clarify where she is in the narrative of her life based on an assessment of what lies behind and what lies ahead. The events of her life again and again force a revision of the story.

Much of *Journal of a Solitude* is concerned with Sarton's struggle, at ages 58 and 59, both to "find herself" and to "change herself." She needs to find herself because she feels like an inadequate machine that breaks down at crucial moments. As noted in Chapter 2, part of her problem is that a false image of herself had been projected in *Plant Dreaming Deep*, that she is not the "wise old party" portrayed there, though the reader gets the sense that it is an image that Sarton convinced herself that she believed. She intends to break through this image to the "rough rocky depths, to the matrix itself" (p. 12). The journal is seen as the vehicle for accomplishing the self-revelation.

She not only wanted to find herself, however. In a somewhat contradictory vein, she writes of wanting to change herself. Change is required because of her "unregenerate, tormenting and tormented self" (p. 12). The idea of changing herself is phrased at several points in the journal in terms of a image of arrested development. She labels herself as immature and writes that the infant must be forced to grow up.

In one of the periods of most intense self-criticism, Sarton offers a description of an external phenomenon that reverberates with her image of herself. Sarton sees a starving, wild cat that has come every day and stared at her with a strange, intense look. Sarton feeds the cat—the cat is so terrified she runs away at once when Sarton opens the door, but comes back to eat ravenously when the door is closed. Sarton senses that the cat's hunger is not only for food—she longs for shelter as well. Sarton asks, as if she were asking of herself, "will she ever become tame enough . . . to give in to what she longs to have?" (p. 57).

The overall movement in the journal is toward greater self-acceptance, although there are numerous rises and falls in this feeling during the year. In a sense she does find herself during the year. In a phrase she quotes from the French writer Louis Lavelle, she takes possession of herself.

> I am proud to be fifty-eight, and still alive and kicking, in love, more creative, balanced, and potent than I have ever been. I mind certain physical deteriorations, but not *really*. (p. 79, emphasis in original)

However, it becomes apparent during the year that much of Sarton's desire to change herself stems from what she felt was required from her love relationship. The decision to break off that relationship and the accompanying decision to leave New Hampshire and move to Maine lifts the obligation she felt to change herself and gives her the sense that she has returned to a deep self that had been "too absorbed and too battered to function" (p. 207). She feels elation at the prospect of her new home and the opportunity to live by the sea.

The House by the Sea was written when Sarton was between ages 62 and 64. In the introduction, she notes that the period between the two journals was marked by intense emotional pain, broken love relationships, and the decline into senility of her long time companion, Judith Matlack. Immediately prior to beginning *The House by the Sea*, she had returned from a trip to Europe during which she had said what in all likelihood were final goodbyes to lifelong friends who were in their 80s and 90s. In various entries between November 1974 and March 1976, Sarton describes the feeling that her life was nearly over. This feeling of life being nearly over is sometimes meant figuratively, sometimes literally. The following quotes from *The House by the Sea* illustrate Sarton's sense during this period that her story had all but come to an end: "It is not only the coming on of winter, but the coming on of old age that I shore up against these days" (p. 35). "[F]or the last few years I have been highly conscious that from now on I am preparing to die, and must think about it, and prepare to do it well" (p. 53). "I am entering a new phase, the simple letting go that means old age" (p. 197); "[t]he deep sense I have of dying and death . . . I feel the heaviness of mortality upon me" (pp. 211–212).

In April 1976, however, the story begins to shift. The shift is precipitated by the stirrings of a new novel. Novels provide an imaginative world which enable her to live her real life with more enthusiasm: "I have longed for an imaginary world in which to live again" (p. 225). With the stirrings of the new novel, which eventually became *A Reckoning*, Sarton feels invigorated: "At last I am beginning to feel some sap in my veins" (p. 232). Writing in April, she makes it clear she now has achieved a certain distance from her previous self-understanding: "What is coming to the surface now is a conglomeration of experiences I have had in the last year . . . most of all, my fear for a short time before Christmas that I might have had a limited life expectancy. . . ." (p. 232). By her 64th birthday on May 3, 1976, there has been a substantial shift in her sense of the narrative moment of her life: "Sixty-four is the best age I have ever been" (p. 245). "I'm calmer and more sure of myself . . . I am happy also because the panic that I would never have another idea for a novel is gone, and I do see my way ahead for another two years" (p. 243). Rather than seeing her life as all but over, she now sees it as stretching out into a future that will yield further generativity.

The failure of *A Reckoning* to achieve critical success and a failed love relationship form the backdrop to *Recovering*, the next journal, which begins two years and four months after the last entry in *The House by the Sea*. On January 5, 1979, at age 66, Sarton sums up the progress of her life.

The worst thing right now is that I no longer have any distant hopes, anything ahead that I look forward to with a leap of the heart. . . . In naked terms, I simply feel a failure. Too old to hope that things will ever get any better. . . . A trajectory, the sense I had of myself and my own powers, has been broken. (pp. 26–27)

Despite the many visits from friends and the flood of letters from admirers, this sense of her life as being figuratively over persists through the next six months. In June, an event occurs that, in Ricoeur's term, is readily configured into this narrative of decline. Sarton is diagnosed with breast cancer and has a mastectomy on June 18, 1979. Initially, she had thought that the real pain might substitute for the mental anguish she had been experiencing. This did not occur; the sense of physical loss attendant to the mastectomy reinforces the sense of loss associated with the critical rejection of her literary work and the pain of the failing love relationship: "I have in the past six months been devalued as a woman, as a lover, and as a writer" (p. 119).

The sense of being at the end of her life persists during the summer months and is dramatically reflected in a dream she reports on July 21.

In the hospital one of the odder things that happened was that I repeatedly woke thinking I was fifty-seven years old, amazed to think I had survived that long, only to realize with a shock that I am actually sixty-seven, ten years older than seems possible! It has been ground into me by the bitter experiences of last year that I am old. (p. 138)

In the entry for September 3, Sarton elaborates on the idea of the future being cut off:

Until now I had felt in a childish way that life was always somewhere ahead preparing suprises, that something amazing was about to happen, and it often did. Now I am coming to understand that my life is over or nearly. The timelessness

at the end approaches. It has been a rich life, filled to the brim
with work and love, and I am really quite ready to let it go.
(p. 180)

And on September 10, in an entry that could be viewed as
the journal's emotional nadir, she wrote: "Why then go on?
Why not give up? . . . I am too old to 'move on' as I could when
I was young and the choices seemed infinite" (p. 186).

Although both the rejection by critics and the mastectomy
are important components of Sarton's tragic narrative, it becomes increasingly clear in the the entries from July to September 1979 that the painful love relationship occupies a
central position in maintaining Sarton's bleak mood. The lifting of the mood and the shift in her self-understanding are
brought about by the decision, recorded on September 13, to
let go of hopes for this relationship, distancing herself from
the love that had proved destructive. As a result, she becomes
reenergized. The mental picture of the trajectory of her life
changed: "[N]ow I am truly on a rising curve. What has
changed in a miraculous way is the landscape of the heart"
(p. 224). The journal concludes in November 1979 with repeated statements that she is wonderfully happy and at ease
with herself, accepting what cannot be changed and going with
instead of against the current.

Two and one half years later at the beginning of the next
journal, *At Seventy*, Sarton still feels her life is on a "rising
curve." Far from feeling that her life was all but over, she felt
that the future still held much for her:

> What is it like to be seventy? If someone else had lived so long
> and could remember things sixty years ago with great clarity,
> she would seem very old to me. But I do not feel old at all. Not
> as much a survivor as a person still on her way. (pp. 9–10)

At a poetry reading, she remarks that this is the best time
of her life and that she loves being old. Someone in the audience incredulously asks, "Why is it good to be old?" Sarton
recorded her answer:

Because I am more myself than I have ever been. There is less
conflict. I am happier, more balanced and (I heard myself say
rather aggressively) "more powerful." (p. 10)

Although she loves being old, she feels young. Sarton repeatedly notes in this journal that she feels younger at 70 than
she did between ages 62 and 64, when she wrote *The House
by the Sea*, or even than she felt at age 60 when she wrote
the poem "Gestalt at Sixty": "It is quite incredible that I am
seventy and feel so young" (p. 272). And what of the earlier
assessment that she had arrived at the end of her life? "Those
previews of old age were not entirely accurate" (p. 37).

An aspect of self-understanding that emerges prominently
in this journal is the idea, introduced in Chapter 4, that one
of the products—and, perhaps, the central product—of Sarton's creative efforts has been the creation of her self.

For Sarton at this point in her life the self is like a much-
valued companion. When this companion is present, Sarton
feels in harmony, she feels like herself; when the companion
is not present, she feels ill at ease. For example, she describes
the feeling of exhaustion after a three-day visit from a friend:

Why then with such a beneficent presence here did I get up so
exhausted? Because the inner life comes to a complete stop.
The self who writes, thinks, gardens, the solitary compulsive
is temporarily absent. (p. 107)

The idea of the presence or absence of her true self is taken
up in the next journal, *After the Stroke*. On February 20, 1986,
at age 73, Sarton suffered a stroke: "I woke in the middle of
the night terrified as I felt as though a numb, perhaps dead,
arm were strangling me. It was actually my left arm. I could
not extricate myself" (p. 23). She knew something was wrong
but went back to bed. In the morning, she went to the hospital and learned that, as she suspected, she'd had a stroke.
The stroke came at a time when she was already dealing with

other illnesses. Beginning during the preceding fall, she had been suffering from incapacitating intestinal cramps. In the course of the testing to determine the cause of the cramps, Sarton learned that she had a fibrillating heart and needed to start taking medication to get the heartbeat back to normal. The medications made her ill. Meanwhile, the cramps persisted.

The period from December 1985 to July 1986 was dominated by Sarton's struggles with her illnesses. The journal documents demoralizing visits to doctors, failed treatments, and hospital stays. The illnesses are configured into the narrative of her life. Now she no longer feels young: "[T]he stroke has made me take the leap into old age instead of approaching it gradually" (p. 35). Along with the feeling of being old is the sense that her real self has departed: "I feel so deprived of my *self*. . . ." (p. 15, emphasis in original). With her self gone, being alone is transformed from a joyful and necessary condition of work to a frightful loneliness.

All during the spring, she is too sick to work. Four months after the stroke she wrote: "To manage such a passive *waiting* life I have had to bury my real self—and now realize that bringing that real self back is going to be even more difficult than it was to bury it" (p. 78).

Fortunately, in the summer of 1986 she begins to experience some improvement. On August 12, Sarton noted that she was beginning to feel herself again. She felt sufficiently improved that she decided to follow through on plans for an ambitious fall lecture tour, which took her to Indianapolis, Bloomington, Albuquerque, San Antonio, Louisville, and Nashville.

For Sarton, feeling better is marked by a return of her self. On August 22, she wrote:

> Because I am well I no longer suffer from the acute loneliness
> I felt all spring and summer until now. Loneliness because in
> spite of all the kindnesses and concern of so many friends there

was no one who could fill the hole at the center of my being—
only myself could fill it by becoming whole again. It was loneliness in essence for the *self*. (p. 124, emphasis in original)

The journal ends one year after the stroke. With the recovery of health, Sarton once again reconfigures the story of her
life. She notes that she has ceased her painful mulling over
the past and is instead dreaming of the future. She is looking
forward to her 75th birthday. She rejoices in the life she has
recaptured and in all that still lies ahead.

The first entry of *Endgame*, the next journal, is May 3, 1990,
Sarton's 78th birthday. Sarton had planned to write a journal that would take her through her seventy-ninth year and
to her 80th birthday. However, mounting health problems
beginning in November 1989 led her to commence another
journal a year earlier than originally anticipated. She changed
her plans and advanced the timing of this journal because
the journal permitted her to stay engaged in at least a mini-
mal form of creativity at a time when she was not capable of
writing either poetry or novels: "In these pathetically dimmed
days the 'one thing' for me is to manage a page a day of this
journal, and when I am unable to write that page I slide back
into a sense of uselessness" (p. 62). As the year progresses,
writing itself becomes impossible, and late in August Sarton
begins to dictate the entries. Sarton may also have decided
to begin another journal earlier than anticipated, because
at the time of her 78th birthday, she may not have been confident she would live to 80. In the event of her death, this
journal would become the final work written during her lifetime.

The health problems documented in this diary are the type
of multiple chronic illnesses faced by many older people. In
Sarton's case, these consisted of a fibrillating heart, irritable
bowel syndrome (diverticulitis), fluid in the lungs, and suspected lung cancer. She is wracked by pain from the diverticulitis, rapidly and unintentionally losing weight—she drops

to 94 pounds—and is weak and frail beyond what she could have imagined possible:

> It's irritating not to be able to walk a straight line, but to fumble, as I walk, to stumble is what I mean, to almost fall so often, and to begin to pant if I walk even twenty yards. It's a strange transformation of a person who used to be quick and volatile and who has now had to become slow and careful—careful not even to feel too much because then I start to cough and feel dizzy. (p. 67)

The journal documents the constant daily presence of chronic illness in the sufferer's life, the struggle not to let the illness dominate every moment, the many hours spent getting to and from doctors' appointments and waiting in doctors' offices, and, most powerfully, the continuous rise and fall of hope.

The idea of the shifting horizon of self-understanding is especially relevant to the internal dialogues of people with chronic illness. As *Endgame* makes powerfully clear, one aspect of the experience of severe chronic illiness is trying to define the present in terms of alternative visions of the future. The struggle to define the present moment in terms of competing imaginings of the future constitutes a dialectic of hope. Days and days of pain despite the doctoring may signify that one's present state is the best that things are going to be, that the future holds nothing of value except more pain and increasing frailty. The loss of hope is evidenced in an entry from July: "I have come to see and to believe that there is no medicine that can help, that I simply must learn to live with it and forget about imagining some doctor might find a solution" (p. 57). At the same time, this thought evokes conflicting thoughts: the idea that maybe the next form of treatment will, indeed, help and the conviction that hope, itself, is a prerequisite for recovery.

The play of the dialectic of hope comes through in *Endgame* especially clearly when Sarton writes about her good days. She asks at many points in the diary whether the good day she is having means that a corner has been turned and that it will be followed by more good days. Repeatedly in this journal, such statements are made; repeatedly, the hope that the corner has been turned is undermined by the return of sleepless nights, pain, and overwhelming lassitude. The reader accompanies Sarton through these oscillations of hope, and, like Sarton, does not know how the story will turn out.

On January 12, 1991, she wrote, "There's no doubt that I'm better. This is what I must cling to—that I *am* better" (p. 202, emphasis in original). Eight days later, the sense of having turned a corner is subverted: "Yesterday was a gloomy day—extremely gloomy—because I thought I had solved my intestinal problem. Instead I had an attack of violent pain" (p. 217). Similarly, after a particularly bad period at the end of February, 1991, on March 1 she wrote: "Today I'm certainly, comparatively speaking, on top of the world. I thought last night when things did go well with my recalcitrant bowel that I might be in for a change for the better. That may be true. Let us hope" (p. 260). But two weeks later the pain has returned ferociously: "I want to die, there's no doubt about that. When you have as much pain as I have and there's no way out you *do* want to die, if you're old as I am. You do want to die" (pp. 277–278, emphasis in original). This low point is followed by another renewal of hope at the end of the journal as Sarton decides to seek help from a practitioner of holistic medicine, whose treatments and dietary regimen do effect an improvement in Sarton's condition.

Under such circumstances, what happens to the sense of self, the self that she has spent her lifetime creating? As in *After the Stroke*, in *Endgame* Sarton comments that during the periods of intense struggle with her illnesses her self departs, that she feels only partly in the world as far as who May Sarton was. Typical of such comments is this entry from June 23, 1990:

If someone found their way here . . . and said they were looking for May Sarton my answer would have to be "she did live
here, but she is not here now." People read books and imagine
I am the person who wrote them sometimes as long as seven-
teen years ago (*Journal of a Solitude*). My values have not
changed and my way of life has changed very little, yet I am no
longer the person who wrote those books. Truly that person
does not live here in the present. (p. 45)

A few weeks later, though, she felt better and was able to
write of the return of the person who had departed: "Lately I
have been slowly re-creating a person, the person I am now,
and so begin to live again" (p. 56) and of the effort required
after her long bout with frustrating illness to be more cheer-
ful and to be "more what I truly think I am" (p. 93).

Endgame ends on May 3, 1991, Sarton's 79th birthday. Her
best birthday present is that she seems to be "better, really
better, at last" (p. 342). The journal itself was a lifesaver, a
relentless pressure, but one that provided a generative project
at a time when her life seemed to have collapsed in on itself.
The reader learns that Sarton intends to go on with the original plan for a journal that will carry her to her eightieth birthday.

The first entry of *Encore*, the next journal, is on May 5, 1991.
Sarton is still very weak and in relentless pain. Yet, during
the year covered in the journal, she repeatedly marshals the
energy to respond to numerous requests for information, to
grant face-to-face interviews, to keep up her voluminous correspondence, and to manage her household. Of utmost significance to her is that during the year, she recovers her ability to write poetry.

The year is highly significant in terms of the continuing
evolution of her self-understanding. She notes that at 80, she
might be happy not reflecting too much on her life and might
rather watch the birds and the ocean. However, this is a year
in which she is forced to think about events from all phases
of her past. The journal records how Sarton is repeatedly

asked to provide remembrances of famous people she has known. She is also involved in reviewing the manuscript for the book *Among the Usual Days*, a selection from her lifetime of correspondence. Finally, she has to come to grips with answering questions from her biographer that explore painful relationships she has not chosen to reveal in her journals. She comments that it is "as if my whole life were constantly pouring through my mind . . ." (p. 108).

During the year, she is also forced to look at herself as the focus of mounting adulation. Several critical studies of her work are written and cited in the journal, as are translations and publication of her work in other countries. There are plans to reissue her collected poems, and contracts for films based on her novels are discussed.

In view of all the forced reminiscence and increased acclaim, what sense of self emerges? That she does think about herself is evident: "[N]othing interests me as much, perhaps, as myself at this stage of my life. I have so much to think about" (p. 168). A major component of the self at this point is that she is old. Because of her illnesses and the constant pain, she cannot ever escape the sense of being old. At one point in the journal she labels herself as an "invalid old lady" (p. 144).

Six months into the journal her unremitting illnesses lead to what she terms "the darkest passage of my life" (p. 145). The foundation of Sarton's life is friendship, and Sarton believes that her friends are getting fed up with her being ill and not getting well. She feels ashamed of herself for acting difficult and cross with friends. "The relentless pain is making the psyche ill as well as the poor old body" (p. 147).

However, of equal prominence is her more solid sense of self-worth and her stronger conviction about the ultimate validity and value of her life than in any of the previous journals. The confirmation of her sense of personal worth arises from many of the year's events. The critical studies, translations, interviews, and possible films have already been mentioned. But there are two particularly powerful events that constitute dramatic public acknowledgments of the value of her life. The first is the presentation to Sarton of a *Festschrift* containing passages of appreciation from distinguished people in arts, literature, and theater. "So I complained about not being recognized! I went through the book with tears streaming down my cheeks, tears of joy, and now I have to say that I *am* recognized, and it makes my heart sing" (p. 253, emphasis in original). The second is a conference at Westbrook College to honor and discuss Sarton's work on the occasion of her 80th birthday. The conference lasts for three days and provides, especially in terms of the acknowledgment of Sarton's poetry, "the accolade I have longed to be given before I die" (p. 325).

At the end of the journal, Sarton declares that she has come through a thicket of ill health and into an extraordinary time of happiness and fulfillment. Her happiness rests on receiving the recognition she has longed for, having a new kind of love realtionship, and earning enough money. But as she looks into the future from the horizon of the present moment, what contributes most to her sense that her true self has returned is the ability to work both on poetry and on the novella she dreams of starting on completion of the journal.

It is difficult to imagine a text or set of texts that documents as clearly and dramatically as Sarton's diaries the movement of the horizon of self-understanding and the changing sense of self that arises as events enter into that horizon and are configured into the story of a life.

As described in the preceding overview of the journals, there is an oscillation during the years covered in the journals between a self-story that is essentially a tragedy (a story in which a hero fails to conquer evil and is excluded from society) and a romance (a story in which an honored past is restored through a series of events that involve the struggle between the hero and the forces of evil).

At any given moment, Sarton did not and could not know what the true story of her life would be. All she could do was attempt to characterize her life, as best she could, from the horizon of the present. The fact that her interpretation of her life changes back and forth from tragedy to romance does not mean that she was deceitful or foolish. Rather, the oscillations in Sarton's constructions of the narrative power of her life reflect a fundamental feature of self-understanding: objectifications of the self, the self-as-known, must always be understood as emerging out of a particular temporal horizon. Even in later life, the movement of that horizon can lead to a reconfiguration of the events of the past and a radical rewriting of the story of one's life.

What Is Knowledge
of Aging Knowledge Of?   9

> *It is remarkable how much consolation and
> hope we can receive from authors who, while
> offering no answers to life's questions, have
> the courage to articulate the situation of their
> lives in all honesty and directness. (Nouwen,
> 1974, p. 35)*

For much of its history, gerontology has assumed that what
we can claim to know about aging emerges exclusively from
the application of the scientific method as traditionally understood: obtaining quantitative measurements of operation-
alized concepts and developing atemporal generalizations
about causal relations.

One problem with following a program of research based
on this assumption is that much data that seems at first blush
to be most germane to understanding aging is excluded from
consideration. The excluded data consists of descriptions by
particular individuals in their own words of the experience of
aging. After all, what can a single person's experience lend to
the scientific study of aging? How can hypothesized causal
relationships be tested with such data? How can we generalize from the single case?

It is impossible to counter these criticisms while working
with the assumption that knowledge is that which emerges
exclusively from the application of the scientific method. The
problem is with the assumption.

To appreciate what is wrong with the assumption that knowledge of aging derives exclusively from application of the scientific method it is helpful to distinguish among three modes of understanding (Runciman, 1983). The first is the understanding necessary to provide a statement of what has been observed to occur. This can be termed *reportage*. The second is the understanding of what caused the situation to occur, or how it came about. This can be termed *explanation*. And the third is the understanding necessary for what can be termed *description*. Description means addressing the question of what it is like to think, feel, say and do something.

To get a sense of each of these three types of understanding, it is helpful to consider a nongerontological example. We could consider, for instance, a wave of strikes. We can conceive of a situation where a report was made about a wave of strikes, a statement of the fact that the strikes had occurred. We can also conceive of putting forward explanations of why the strikes came about, the causes of the strikes. But is that all that we should expect strike researchers to concern themselves with? There is more to the strikes than the fact that they occurred and the hypothesized causes. It is perfectly legitimate to seek some understanding of what it was like for those who were motivated to go on strike under the reported conditions. What did they think they were doing? What were their ideas of their relations with their co-workers, supervisors, and union officials? What was their sense of the grievance to which they were giving expression? In other words, what was the meaning of the strikes to those who participated in them, or, using the term introduced in Chapter 1, what was the *lived* experience of the strikes? The researcher who is unable to answer such questions cannot be said to fully know about the wave of strikes.

In gerontology, there is a bias toward identifying knowledge of aging with the categories of reportage and explanation. We want to know the facts about older people and the aging process and we want explanations of causes. How many speeches have been given and how many pamphlets written about the myths versus the realities of aging? Descriptions of the meanings of aging cannot be proved. They may be viewed as providing artistic flourishes to scientific accounts, but according to the usual way of thinking, in no way do they constitute a form of knowledge in their own right.

This bias is reflected in the popularity of and research on Palmore's (1988) Facts on Aging Quiz. Scores on the Facts on Aging Quiz are used to provide an operational definition of knowledge of aging. Under this definition, subjects who score high on this test are defined as knowing more about aging than subjects who do not score high. Although the value of Palmore's quizzes as a heuristic device and as a means of prompting discussion cannot be disputed, there is considerable question about using this test to represent knowledge of aging. Older people themselves, such as the diarists considered in this book, may score low on Palmore's test, yet would we wish to assert, without qualification, that they have little knowledge of aging?

Knowledge of aging consists not only of reports about facts and explanations of causes but also of descriptions of the meanings people create out of the experiences associated with growing older. Once we acknowledge that descriptions of age-related experiences are part of knowledge of aging, the value of personal journals as a source of such descriptions becomes readily apparent.

The philosophical tradition of hermeneutics teaches us that the descriptions that people provide of their own aging are not theirs alone. They shared. Older individuals' descriptions of their experiences emerge out of the way the experience of aging has been framed in the past, the history of meanings attached to the struggles of later life. The published journals discussed in this book constitute events in that history. They emerged out of the history of our understanding of the meaning of aging, and they now are a part of that history.

The shared nature of the descriptions offered in the journals derives in part from the obvious fact that interpretations
offered in them are carried out linguistically. As individuals,
we do not have language. Rather, we enter into language in
our early years and for the rest of life are participants in linguistic traditions. We belong to language as much as language
belongs to us.

Because of the shared nature of language, whenever people
express themselves linguistically, there is a sense in which it
is not solely those individuals' 'experiences that are being
expressed. When people write about what they feel, what a
particular incident in their lives—such as a hospitalization
or an encounter with a bag lady—means to them, they draw
on the means-at-hand, the available words and concepts to
express themselves. As Palmer has put it, "experience, thinking, and understanding are linguistic through and through"
(1969, p. 203). We talk about being true to ourselves and the
uniqueness of every person's experience, but tend to overlook
the way in which, because of the shared nature of language
through which experience is constituted, no one's experience
is unique.

The process of aging is not just a matter of changes in the
functioning of our bodies and concomitant changes in psychological functioning. The process of aging is in part a historical process involving not only the history of social policy
toward the aged, but, equally, the history of older people's
understandings of themselves. When people age, they are
necessarily involved in this historical process, the evolving
history of the meaning of later life. The interpretations of
aging offered in journals of later life should be studied, because such interpretations are as much a part of the process of aging as the behavior of free radicals or changes in
reaction time.

The study of journals of later life, as opposed to the writing
of the journals, sets up a double hermeneutic. The journal

writer is engaged in a hermeneutic process in offering linguistic expressions of his or her experience. The gerontologist who studies the journal and offers an account of what the journal means is also involved in a hermeneutic process. What kind of knowledge is it that emerges from the interpretation of interpretations? What makes an interpretation of a journal correct?

The study of personal journals of later life will not generate timeless truths. The encounter of the gerontologically minded reader with the published text is itself an historical event. The interpretations offered necessarily are influenced by the interpreter's forestructures of understanding, which themselves derive from a particular historical moment and set of concerns. The most we can achieve is to enter into a dialogue with the text in which we attempt to hear what is in the text and, in Gadamer's term, *fuse* the writer's horizon of understanding with that of the reader. Clearly, the understanding we have of these texts will change over time as the historical circumstances of readers changes. Nonetheless, the fact that the knowledge we have of the texts considered in this book is temporally contingent does not mean that it is not knowledge. Such time-bound knowledge is simply all that we can ever achieve in attempting to grasp expressions of life.

The readings of the personal journals presented in the preceding chapters are not offered as the sole correct readings of these texts. There are no objective, timeless truths about the meaning of texts. They are intended, rather, as opening remarks in what, I hope, will become a hermeneutical dialogue in gerontology about these works. Valid interpretation emerges from dialogue about the meaning of texts within an interpretive community of like-minded readers.

The study of personal journals allows us to hold up for examination the ways that people have responded to the human situation in the later years—individuals who, while offering no answers to life's questions, have had the courage to articulate the situation of their lives in all honesty and directness and have grappled with the challenge of maintaining a sense of meaningfulness in the face of the inevitable losses of aging. As we take possession of these works in the field of gerontology, we have the opportunity to help older people live more enriched and fully potentiated lives.

References

Abbott, H. (1984). *Diary fiction: Writing as action*. Ithaca, NY: Cornell University Press.

Ainsworth, M. D. S. (1989). Attachments beyond infancy. *American Psychologist*, *44*, 709–716.

Allport, G. W. (1942). *The use of personal documents in psychological science*. New York: Social Science Research Council.

Allport, G. W. (1965). *Letters from Jenny*. New York: Harcourt, Brace & World.

Allport, G. W., Bruner, J. S., & Jandorf, E. M. (1941). Personality under social catastrophe: An analysis of German refugees' life stories. *Character and Personality*, *10*, 1–22.

Atchley, R. C. (1971). Retirement and leisure participation: Continuity or crisis? *The Gerontologist*, *11*, 13–17.

Bakan, D. (1966). *The duality of human existence: An essay on psychology and religion*. Chicago: Rand McNally.

Bakerman, J. (1982). Patterns of love and friendship: Five novels by May Sarton. In C. Hunting (Ed.), *May Sarton: Woman and Poet* Orono, ME: National Poetry Foundation—University of Maine at Orono.

Baldwin, A. L. (1940). The statistical analysis of the structure of a single personality. *Psychological Bulletin*, *37*, 518–519.

201

Baldwin, A. L. (1942). Personal structure analysis: A statistical method for investigating the single personality. *Journal of Abnormal and Social Psychology, 37*, 163–183.

Baltes, P., Smith, J., Staudinger, U., & Sowarka, D. (1990). Wisdom: One facet of successful aging? In M. Perlmutter (Ed.), *Late life potential* Washington, DC: The Gerontological Society of America.

Barbellion, W. N. P. (1984). *Journal of a disappointed man & A last diary*. London: Hogarth Press (original works published 1919 and 1920).

Becker, E. (1973). *The denial of death*. New York: Free Press.

Belenky, M. F., Clinchy, B. M., Goldberger, N. R., & Tarule, J. M. (1986). *Women's ways of knowing: the development of self, voice and mind*. New York: Basic Books.

Bengtson, V. L., Reddy, M. N., & Gordon, C. (1985). Aging and self-conceptions: Personality processes and social contexts. In J. E. Birren & K. W. Schaie (Eds.), *Handbook of the psychology of aging*, (pp. 544–593). New York: Van Nostrand.

Benstock, S. (1988). Authorizing the autobiographical. In S. Benstock (Ed.), *The private self: Theory and practice of women's autobiographical writing* (pp. 10–33). Chapel Hill, NC: University of North Carolina Press.

Blouin, L. P. (1978). *May Sarton: A bibliography*. Metuchen, NJ: The Scarecrow Press.

Blumer, H. (1939). *Critiques of research in the social sciences I: An appraisal of Thomas and Znaniecki's the Polish Peasant in Europe and America*. New York: Social Science Research Council.

Bowlby, J. (1988). *A secure base: Parent-child attachment and healthy human development*. New York: Basic Books.

Bridgman, P. (1927). *The logic of modern physics*. New York: Macmillan.

Bruner, J. (1987). Life as narrative. *Social Research, 54*, 11–32.

Bruner, J. (1990). *Acts of meaning*. Cambridge, MA: Harvard University Press.

Bruyn, S. T. (1966). *The human perspective in sociology: the methodology of participant observation*. Englewood Cliffs, NJ: Prentice Hall.

Buehler, C. (1935). The curve of life as studied in biographies. *Journal of Applied Psychology, 19*, 405–409.

Buehler, C., & Massarik, F. (Eds.) (1968). *The course of human life.* New York: Springer.

Burke, R. (1992, June). Interpretive reasoning. Paper presented at International Human Science Research Conference, Rochester, MI.

Chodorow, N. (1978). *The reproduction of mothering: Psychoanalysis and the sociology of gender.* Berkeley, CA: University of California Press.

Chodorow, N. (1989). *Feminism and psychoanalytic theory.* New Haven, CT: Yale University Press.

Cohler, B. J. (1982). Personal narrative and life-course. In P. B. Baltes & O. G. Brim (Eds.), *Life span development and behavior* (pp. 205–241). New York: Academic Press.

Cohler, B. J., & Galatzer-Levy, R. M. (1990). Self, meaning and morale across the second half of life. In R. A. Nemiroff & C. A. Colarusso (Eds.), *New dimensions in adult development* (pp. 214–263). New York: Basic Books.

Cole, T. R., & Gadow, S. A. (Eds.) (1986). *What does it mean to grow old: Reflections from the humanities.* Durham, NC: Duke University Press.

Cole, T. R., Van Tassel, D. D., & Kastenbaum, R. (Eds.). (1992). *Handbook of the humanities and aging.* New York: Springer.

Dannefer, D., Perlmutter, M. (1990). Development as a multi-dimensional process: Individual and social constituents. *Human Development, 33,* 108–137.

Denzin, N. K. (1989a). *Interpretive biography.* Newbury Park, CA: Sage.

Denzin, N. K. (1989b). *Interpretive interactionism.* Newbury Park, CA: Sage.

Derrida, J. (1978). *Writing and difference.* Chicago: University of Chicago Press (original work published 1967).

Dinnage, R. (1984, November 8). Review of V. Woolf's diaries. *New York Review of Books,* 3–4.

Dinnerstein, D. (1977). *The mermaid and the minotaur: Sexual arrangements and human malaise.* New York: Harper & Row.

Espin, O. M., Stewart, A. J., & Gomez, C. A. (1990). Letters from V: Adolescent personality development in sociohistorical context. *Journal of Personality, 58,* 347–364.

Faulconer, J. E., & Williams, R. N. (1985). Temporality in human action: An alternative to positivism and historicism. *American Psychologist, 40,* 1179–1188.

Fingarette, H. (1963). *The self in transformation.* New York: Harper & Row.

Fothergill, R. A. (1974). *Private chronicles: A study of English diaries.* London: Oxford University Press.

Frankl, V. E. (1959). *Man's search for meaning: An introduction to logotherapy.* New York: Washington Square Press.

Frankl, V. E. (1963). *Man's search for meaning.* New York: Washington Square Press.

Frankl, V. E. (1969). *The will to meaning.* New York: New American Library.

Frankl, V. E. (1971). *The doctor and the soul* (2nd ed.). New York: Bantam Books.

Frankl, V. E. (1978). *The unheard cry for meaning: Psychotherapy and humanism.* New York: Simon & Schuster.

Franz, C. E., & White, K. M. (1985). Individuation and attachment in personality development: Extending Erikson's theory. *Journal of Personality, 53,* 224–256.

Freeman, M. (1993). *Rewriting the self: History, memory, narrative.* London: Routledge.

Freud, S. (1904). Dichtung und Wahrheit. In J. Strachey (Ed.), *The Standard Edition of the Complete Psychological Works of Sigmund Freud.* London: Hogarth.

Freud, S. (1907). Den Wahn und die Traumeim W. Jensen's Gradiva. In J. Strachey (Ed.), *The Standard Edition of the Complete Psychological Works of Sigmund Freud.* London: Hogarth.

Freud, S. (1911). Psychoanalytic notes upon an autobiographical account of a case of paranoia (dementia paranoides). In J. Strachey (Ed.), *The Standard Edition of the Complete Psychological Works of Sigmund Freud.* London: Hogarth.

Freud, S. (1949). *Outline of psychoanalysis.* New York: Norton.

Frye, N. (1957). *Anatomy of criticism.* Princeton, NJ: Princeton University Press.

Gadamer, H.-G. (1992). *Truth and method* (J. Weinsheimer & D. G. Marshall, Trans.). (Second, Revised ed.). New York: Crossroad (original work published 1960).

Gagnon, J. H. (1992). The self, its voices, and their discord. In C. Ellis & M. G. Flaherty (Eds.), *Investigating subjectivity: Re-*

search on lived experience (pp. 221–243). Newbury Park, CA: Sage.

Gay, P. (1988). *Freud: A life for our time.* New York: Norton.

Geertz, C. (1973). *The interpretation of culture.* New York: Basic Books.

Geertz, C. (1979). From the native's point of view: On the nature of anthropological understanding. In P. Rabinow & W. M. Sullivan (Eds.), *Interpretive social science: A reader* (pp. 225–241). Berkeley, CA: University of California Press.

Geertz, C. (1980). Blurred genres: The refiguration of social thought. *American Scholar* (Spring), 165–179.

Gergen, K. J. (1980). The emerging crisis in life-span developmental theory. In P. B. Baltes & O. G. Brim Jr. (Eds.), *Life-span development and behavior* (pp. 31–63). New York: Academic Press.

Gergen, K. J., & Gergen, M. M. (1983). Narratives of the self. In T. R. Sarbin & K. E. Scheibe (Eds.), *Studies in social identity* (pp. 254–273). New York: Praeger.

Gergen, K. J., & Gergen, M. M. (1988). Narrative and the self as relationship. *Advances in Experimental Social Psychology, 31,* 17–56.

Gilligan, C. (1982). *In a different voice: Psychological theory and women's development.* Boston: Harvard University Press.

Giorgi, A. (1970). *Psychology as a human science.* New York: Harper & Row.

Goldbrunner, J. (1964). *Individuation: A study of the depth psychology of Carl Gustav Jung.* Notre Dame, IN: Notre Dame University Press.

Goldman, C. (1988). *Late bloomers: Stories of successful aging.* Fairfax Station, VA: Connie Goldman Productions.

Gottschalk, L., Kluckhohn, C., & Angell, R. (1942). *The use of personal documents in history, anthropology and sociology.* New York: Social Science Research Council.

Grumbach, D. (1991). *Coming into the end zone.* New York: Norton.

Grumbach, D. (1993). *Extra innings.* New York: Norton.

Gubrium, J. (1993). *Speaking of life: Horizons of meaning for nursing home residents.* Hawthorne, NY: Aldine de Gruyter.

Gubrium, J. F. (1975). *Living and dying at Murray Manor.* New York: St. Martin's Press.

Gubrium, J. F. (Ed.). (1976). *Time, roles and self in old age.* New York: Behavioral Publications.

Gubrium, J. F. (1986). *Oldtimer's and Alzheimer's: The descriptive organization of senility.* Greenwich, CT: JAI Press.

Gubrium, J. F. (1992). Qualitative research comes of age in gerontology. *The Gerontologist, 32,* 581–582.

Gusdorf, G. (1980). Conditions and limits of autobiography. In J. Olney (Ed.), *Autobiography: Essays theoretical and critical* (pp. 28–48). Princeton: Princeton University Press.

Gutmann, D. (1987). *Reclaimed powers: Toward a new psychology of men and women in later life.* New York: Basic Books.

Hall, G. S. (1904). *Adolescence.* New York: Appleton.

Harter, S. (1983). Developmental perspectives on the self-system. In E. M. Hetherington (Ed.), *Handbook of child psychology* (pp. 275–385). New York: Wiley.

Haviland, J. M., & Kramer, D. A. (1991). Affect-cognition relationships in adolescent diaries: The case of Anne Frank. *Human Development, 34,* 143–159.

Housman, A. E. (1965). The collected poems of A. E. Housman. New York: Holt, Rinehart and Winston. (original work published, 1896)

Hunting, C. (Ed.). (1982). *Mary Sarton: Woman and poet.* Orono, ME: University of Maine at Orono.

Hunting, C. (1986). May Sarton. In P. Quartermain (Ed.), *Dictionary of literary biography* (pp. 376–386). Detroit, MI: Gale Research.

James, W. (1901). *The varieties of religious experience.* New York: Modern Library.

James, W. (1961). *Psychology: The briefer course.* New York: Harper & Brothers. (original work published 1892)

Jung, C. G. (1933). *Modern man in search of a soul* (W. S. Dell & C. F. Baynes, Trans.). New York: Harcourt Brace Jovanovich.

Kastenbaum, R. (1964). *New thoughts on old age.* New York: Springer.

Kastenbaum, R. (1973). Epilogue: Loving, dying, and other gerontologic addenda. In C. Eisdorfer & M. P. Lawton (Eds.), *The psychology of adult development and aging* (pp. 699–708). Washington, DC: American Psychological Association.

Kastenbaum, R. (1992). The creative process: A life-span approach. In T. R. Cole, D. D. Van Tassel, & R. Kastenbaum (Eds.), *Handbook of the humanities and aging* (pp. 285–306). New York: Springer.

Kaufman, S. R. (1986). *The ageless self: Sources of meaning in later life*. Madison, WI: University of Wisconsin Press.

Kegan, R. (1982). *The evolving self*. Cambridge, MA: Harvard University Press.

Kotre, J. (1984). *Outliving the self: Generativity and the interpretation of lives*. Baltimore: Johns Hopkins University Press.

Kuypers, J. A. (1977). Aging: Potentials for personal liberation. *Humanitas*, 17–38.

Laing, R. D. (1966). *Interpersonal perception*. New York: Springer.

Latham, R. (Ed.). (1983). *The illustrated Pepys: Extracts from the diary*. Berkeley, CA: University of California Press.

Levinson, D., Darrow, C. N., Klein, E. B., Levinson, M. H., & McKee, B. (1978). *Seasons of a man's life*. New York: Knopf.

Levinson, D. J. (1980). Toward a conception of the adult life course. In N. Smelser & E. H. Erikson (Eds.), *Themes of love and work in adulthood* (pp. 265–290). Cambridge, MA: Harvard University Press.

Levinson, D. J. (1981). Explorations in biography. In A. L. Rabin, J. Aronoff, A. M. Barclay, & R. A. Zucker (Eds.), *Further explorations in personality* (pp. 44–79). New York: Wiley.

Levinson, D. J. (1986). A conception of adult development. *American Psychologist, 41*, 3–13.

Maas, H., & Kuypers, J. A. (1974). *From thirty to seventy*. San Francisco: Jossey-Bass.

Maddi, S. R. (1970). The search for meaning. In W. J. Arnold & M. M. Page (Eds.), *Nebraska symposium on motivation* (pp. 137–186). Lincoln, NE: University of Nebraska Press.

Mahler, M. S., Pine, F., & Bergman, A. (1975). *The psychological birth of the human infant: Symbiosis and individuation*. New York: Basic Books.

Mahoney, M. (1991). *Human change processes: The scientific foundations of psychotherapy*. New York: Basic Books.

Mallon, T. (1984). *A book of one's own: People and their diaries*. New York: Ticknor and Fields.

Matthews, W. (1950). *British diaries: An annotated bibliography of British diaries written between 1442 & 1942*. Berkeley: University of California Press.

Matuz, R. (Ed.). (1991). *Contemporary literary criticism*. Detroit: Gale Research.

McAdams, D. P. (1988). *Power, intimacy and the life story*. New York: Guilford.

McAdams, D. P. (1993). *The stories we live by*. New York: William Morrow.

Mishler, E. (1986). The analysis of interview-narratives. In T. R. Sarbin (Ed.), *Narrative psychology: The storied nature of human conduct* (pp. 233–255). New York: Praeger.

Moffett, J. (1985). *Points of departure: An anthology of nonfiction*. New York: New American Library.

Moody, H. R. (1988). Toward a critical gerontology: The contribution of the humanities to theories of aging. In J. E. Birren & V. L. Bengtson (Eds.), *Emergent theories of aging* (pp. 19–40). New York: Springer.

Moore, B. E., & Fine, B. D. (Eds.). (1990). *Psychoanalytic terms and concepts*. New Haven, CT: Yale University Press.

Murray, K. (1989). The construction of identity in the narratives of romance and comedy. In J. Schotter & K. J. Gergen (Eds.), *Texts of identity* (pp. 176–205). London: Sage.

Neugarten, B. (1968). Awareness of middle age. In B. Neugarten (Ed.), *Middle age and aging* (pp. 93–98). Chicago: University of Chicago Press.

Neugarten, B. (1973). Personality change in later life. In C. Eisdorfer & M. P. Lawton (Eds.), *The psychology of adult development and aging* (pp. 311–355). Washington, DC: American Psychological Association.

Neugarten, B. (1985). Interpretive social science and research on aging. In A. S. Rossi (Ed.), *Gender and the life course* (pp. 291–300). New York: Aldine.

Neugarten, B. L., & Hagestad, G. O. (1976). Age and the life course. In R. H. Binstock & E. Shanas (Eds.), *Handbook of aging and the social sciences* (pp. 35–55). New York: Van Nostrand Reinhold.

Nouwen, H. J. M. (1974). *Out of solitude: Three meditations on Christian life*. Notre Dame, IN: Ave Maria Press.

Nussbaum, F. A. (1988). Toward conceptualizing diary. In J. Olney (Ed.), *Studies in autobiography* (pp. 128–140). New York: Oxford University Press.

Packer, M. J., & Addison, R. B. (Eds.). (1989). *Entering the circle:*

Hermeneutic investigation in psychology. Albany, NY: State University of New York Press.

Palmer, R. E. (1969). *Hermeneutics*. Evanston, IL: Northwestern University Press.

Palmore, E. B. (1988). *The facts on aging quiz: A handbook of uses and results*. New York: Springer.

Pascal, B. (1950). *Pascal's Pensée's* (H. F. Stewart, Trans.) New York: Pantheon.

Pepys, S. (1970–1973). *The diary of Samuel Pepys*. Berkeley: University of California.

Peterson, B. E., & Stewart, A. J. (1990). Using personal and fictional documents to assess psychosocial development: A case study of Vera Brittain's generativity. *Psychology and Aging*, *5*, 400–411.

Pike, K. (1967). *Language in relation to a unified theory of the structure of human behavior* (2nd ed.). The Hague: Mouton and Co.

Plummer, K. (1983). *Documents of life*. London: Allen and Unwin.

Pocklinghorne, D. E. (1983). *Methodology for the human sciences*. Albany, NY: State University of New York Press.

Polisar, D., Wygant, L., Cole, T., & Perdomo, C. (Eds.). (1988). *Where do we come from? What are we? Where are we going?: An annotated bibliography of aging and the humanities*. Washington, DC: Gerontological Society of America.

Ponsonby, A. (1922). *English Diaries: A review of English diaries from the sixteenth to the twentieth century with an introduction on diary writing*. New York: George H. Doran.

Ponsonby, A. (1927). *More English diaries: Further reviews of diaries from the sixteenth to the twentieth century with an introduction on diary reading*. New York: George H. Doran.

Progoff, I. (1975). *At a journal workshop: The basic text and guide for using the intensive journal*. New York: Dialogue House Library.

Rabinow, P., & Sullivan, W. (Eds.). (1979). *Interpretive social science: A reader*. Berkeley: University of California Press.

Rabinow, P., & Sullivan, W. M. (Eds.). (1987). *Interpretive social science: A second look*. Berkeley: University of California Press.

Rainer, T. (1978). *The new diary: How to use a journal for self-guidance and expanded creativity*. Los Angeles: J. P. Tarcher.

Reinharz, S., & Rowles, G. (1988a). Qualitative gerontology: Themes and challenges. In S. Reinharz & G. Rowles (Eds.), *Qualitative gerontology* (pp. 3–33). New York: Springer.

Reinharz, S., & Rowles, G. D. (Eds.). (1988b). *Qualitative gerontology*. New York: Springer.

Reker, G. T., & Wong, P. T. P. (1988). Aging as an individual process: Toward a theory of personal meaning. In J. E. Birren & V. L. Bengtson (Eds.), *Emergent theories of aging*. New York: Springer.

Ricoeur, P. (1981). *Hermeneutics and the human sciences* (J. B. Thompson, Trans.). Cambridge: Cambridge University Press.

Ricoeur, P. (1992). *Oneself as another* (K. Blamey, Trans.). Chicago: University of Chicago Press.

Rorty, A. O. (1976). A literary postscript: Characters, persons, selves, individuals. In A. O. Rorty (Ed.), *The identities of persons*. Berkeley: University of California Press.

Rosenberg, S., & Jones, R. A. (1972). A method for investigating and representing a person's implicit theory of personality. *Journal of Personality and Social Psychology, 22*, 372–386.

Runciman, W. G. (1983). *A treatise on social theory*. Cambridge: Cambridge University Press.

Ryff, C. (1989). In the eye of the beholder: Views of psychological well-being among middle aged and younger adults. *Psychology and Aging, 4*, 195–210.

Sacks, S. (1967). *Fiction and the shape of belief*. Berkeley: University of California Press.

Sampson, E. E. (1985). The decentralization of identity: Toward a revised concept of personal and social order. *American Psychologist, 40*, 1203–1211.

Sarbin, T. R. (Ed.) (1986). *Narrative psychology: The storied nature of human conduct*. New York: Praeger.

Sarton, M. (1968). *Plant dreaming deep*. New York: Norton.

Sarton, M. (1970). *Kinds of love*. New York: Norton.

Sarton, M. (1973a). *As we are now*. New York: Norton.

Sarton, M. (1973b). *Journal of a solitude*. New York: Norton.

Sarton, M. (1977). *The house by the sea: A journal*. New York: Norton.

Sarton, M. (1980a). *Recovering: A journal*. New York: Norton.

Sarton, M. (1980b). *Writings on writing*. Orono, ME: Puckerbrush Press.

Sarton, M. (1984). *At seventy: A journal*. New York: Norton.

Sarton, M. (1988). *After the stroke*. New York: Norton.

Sarton, M. (1992). *Endgame: A journal of the seventy-ninth year*. New York: Norton.

Sarton, M. (1993). *Encore: A journal of the eightieth year*. New York: Norton.

Sass, L. A. (1988). Humanism, hermeneutics and the concept of the human subject. In S. B. Messer, L. A. Sass, & R. L. Woolfolk (Eds.), *Hermeneutics and psychological theory*. New Brunswick: Rutgers University.

Schafer, R. (1976). *A new language for psychoanalysis*. New Haven: Yale University Press.

Schleuter, P., & Schleuter, J. (Eds.). (1988). *An encyclopedia of British women writers*. New York: Garland Press.

Schlissel, L. (1982). *Women's diaries of the westward journey*. New York: Schocken.

Schulz, J. (1992). *The economics of aging* (5th ed.). Dover, DE: Auburn House.

Schwartz, H., & Jacobs, J. (1979). *Qualitative sociology: A method to the madness*. London: Collier-Macmillan.

Sears, R. R. (1979, June). Mark Twain's separation anxiety. *Psychology Today*, pp. 100–104.

Sheehy, G. (1976). *Passages: Predictable crisis of adult life*. New York: Dutton.

Sherman, E. (1991). *Reminiscence and the self in old age*. New York: Springer.

Shotter, J., & Gergen, K. (Eds.). (1989). *Texts of identity*. London: Sage.

Sibley, A. (1972). *May Sarton*. New York: Twayne.

Smith, S. (1987). *A poetics of women's autobiography: Marginality and the fictions of self-representation*. Bloomington, IN: Indiana University Press.

Spacks, P. (1976). *Imagining a self: Autobiography and novel in eighteenth century England*. Cambridge, MA: Harvard University Press.

Spence, D. P. (1989). Rhetoric vs. evidence as a source of persuasion: A critique of the case study genre. In M. J. Packer & R. B. Addison (Eds.), *Entering the circle: Hermeneutic investigation in psychology* (pp. 205–221). Albany, NY: State University of New York Press.

Spicker, S. F., Woodward, K. M., & Van Tassel, D. D. (Eds.). (1978). *Aging and the elderly: Humanistic perspectives in gerontology.* Atlantic Highlands, NJ: Humanities Press, Inc.

Stauffer, D. (1930). *The art of English biography before 1700.* Cambridge, MA: Harvard University Press.

Stewart, A. J., Frantz, C., & Layton, L. (1988). The changing self: Using personal documents to study lives. *Journal of Personality, 56*, 41–74.

Storr, A. (1988). *Solitude: A return to the self.* New York: Free Press.

Suls, J. M., & Wills, T. A. (Eds.) (1991). *Social comparison: Contemporary theory and research.* Hillsdale, NJ: Lawrence Erlbaum and Associates.

Thomas, L. E. (1989). The human science approach to understanding adulthood and aging. In L. E. Thomas (Ed.), *Research on adulthood and aging: The human science approach* (pp. 1–7). Albany, NY: State University of New York Press.

Thomas, W. I., & Znaniecki, F. (1958). *The Polish peasant in Europe and America.* New York: Dover (original works published 1918–1920).

Tobin, S. S. (1991). *Personhood in advanced old age: Implications for practice.* New York: Springer.

Trilling, L. (1972). *Sincerity and authenticity.* Cambridge, MA: Harvard University Press.

Updike, J. (1975). *A month of Sundays.* New York: Knopf.

Van Manen, M. (1990). *Researching lived experience.* London, Canada: Althouse Press.

Vining, E. G. (1970). *Quiet pilgrimage.* Philadelphia: J. B. Lippincott.

Vining, E. G. (1978). *Being seventy: The measure of a year.* New York: Viking.

Viorst, J. (1986). *Necessary losses.* New York: Ballantine Books.

Watzlawick, P. (Ed.). (1984). *The invented reality: Contributions to constructivism.* New York: Norton.

Weintraub, K. (1978). *The value of the individual: Self and circumstance in autobiography.* Chicago: University of Chicago Press.

Wertz, F. (1984). Procedures in phenomenological research and the question of validity. In M. Anastoos (Ed.), *Exploring the lived world: Readings in phenomenological psychology.* Carrollton,

GA: West Georgia College Studies in the Social Sciences, *23*,
29–48.

Wiersma, J. (1992). Karen: The transforming story. In G. C. Rosen-
wald & R. L. Ochberg (Eds.), *Storied lives: The cultural politics
of self-understanding* (pp. 195–213). New Haven, CT: Yale University Press.

Woolfolk, R. L., Sass, L. A., & Messer, S. B. (1988). Introduction to
hermeneutics. In S. B. Messer, L. A. Sass, & R. L. Woolfolk
(Eds.), *Hermeneutics and psychological theory* (pp. 2–26). New
Brunswick, NJ: Rutgers University Press.

Wrightsman, L. S. (1981). Personal documents as data in conceptualizing adult personality development. *Personality and Social
Psychology Bulletin, 7*, 367–385.

Wrightsman, L. S. (1988). *Personality development in adulthood.*
Beverly Hills, CA: Sage.

Yahnke, R. E., & Eastman, R. M. (1990). *Aging in literature: A
reader's guide.* Chicago: American Library Association.

Yalom, I. D. (1980). *Existential psychotherapy.* New York: Basic
Books.

Yalom, I. D. (1989). *Love's executioner & other tales of psychotherapy.* New York: Basic Books.

Index

215